PRAISE

"Melissa has a unique perspective of overcoming her obstacles to glorify God. Her unconditional love for her son is a true beauty. Her story about having a positive attitude is the best gift for anyone who is about to lose hope, because her words encourage us to keep listening to our hearts and follow God's plans with grateful hearts, no matter how difficult the challenges we face."

Heather Whitestone McCallum
Miss America 1995, Author and Motivational Speaker

"Forever blessed that God brought the light that is Melissa Young into my life, I immediately knew she was someone special. Her story is irrevocably inspiring, and she has taught me to always choose forgiveness because we don't know when the Lord will call us home."

Amanda Hughes,
2019 Orange County (CA) Young Republican President

"Melissa Young embodies the spirit of a warrior and true patriot to this nation. Her determination to allow nothing to stop her from living and loving is an inspiration to millions. Melissa's role in support of President Trump early during his 2016 historic presidential campaign blessed so many women in this nation. Her outer and inner beauty truly shines the light of Jesus Christ, Our Savior."

Pastor Mark Burns
Renowned motivational speaker
Labeled by TIME magazine as 'Donald Trump's Top Pastor'

PRAISE

"Melissa Young is the epitome of strength, the poster child for patriotism and the absolute symbolism of hope. The example she sets for her amazing son is a personal admiration I have for her and she is an incredible inspiration to me. Although faced with an inevitable and heartbreaking future, she has taught him how to cherish each moment in life as if it's the last. Melissa's tenacity to keep fighting and live life to the fullest is a virtue all of us should possess. It is an incredible honor to call her my friend and to share such a powerful common love for our country and family."

Kimberly Munley SGT (R)
Fort Hood Police Department
National Hero, Awarded the 'Defense of Freedom' Medal

Something Beautiful is Going to Happen . . .

My Incredible Story of Fierce Devotion Embracing God, a Son, and Life Itself

Melissa Young

Joshua Tree
Publishing

• Chicago •

Something Beautiful is Going to Happen . . .
My Incredible Story of Fierce Devotion
Embracing God, a Son, and Life Itself
Melissa Young

Published by
Joshua Tree Publishing
• Chicago •
JoshuaTreePublishing.com

13-Digit ISBN: 978-1-941049-99-0

Front Cover Image Credit: © Kevin J. Garay.

Scripture from: New International Version (NIV) Holy Bible, New International Version®, NIV® Copyright ©1973, 1978, 1984, 2011 by Biblica, Inc.® Used by permission. All rights reserved worldwide.

Disclaimer:
This book is designed to provide information about the subject matter covered. The opinions and information expressed in this book are those of the author, not the publisher. Every effort has been made to make this book as complete and as accurate as possible. However, there may be mistakes both typographical and in content. Therefore, this text should be used only as a general guide and not as the ultimate source of information. The author and publisher of this book shall have neither liability nor responsibility to any person or entity with respect to any loss or damage caused or alleged to be caused directly or indirectly by the information contained in this book.

Printed in the United States of America

To my sweet Jack

If you ever need me and I am not within reach, look for me here. This is where you will find me. I'm speaking to you through the pages of this book. My voice and presence will be clear. I can picture your beautiful brown eyes reading this now, and it brings me a joyful smile. Speaking of those beautiful brown eyes, keep them upon God. Follow that small, still voice within—that is the voice of Him. Like Paul said, "Walk by faith, not by sight." Know that you are being led, but if you ever feel that you've lost your way, rest in the loving arms of God and His grace will carry you home. Stand tall, but if you fall, let it be on your knees. Pray to God. Pray a lot. He holds the key to your every need.

My greatest blessing was being chosen to be your mother. You will always be the boy who forever occupied my heart and gave me super powers to fight on. You are a ray of sunshine. Continue to share your bright aura with the world; it's a gift to all. As President Trump said, you are "absolutely magnificent." Aim for the stars, Jack, because that's where you belong. You are my light, my life, my purpose, my fight, and above all, YOU ARE LOVED! Shine on, my son.

To the moon and back,
Mommy

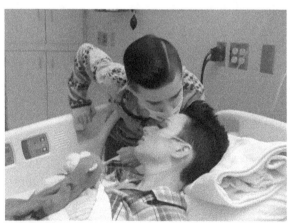

"In the same way, let your light shine before others, that they may see your good deeds and glory to your Father in heaven." Matthew 5:16

TABLE OF CONTENTS

FOREWORD

What really matters in my life? What do I believe at my core? How do I handle adversity? What am I willing to fight for?

These questions were racing through my mind as my plane soared through the night sky at thirty thousand feet late one warm June evening. Each had been stirred in me as I listened to the stories told by the beauty queen who occupied seat B in row 35 right next to me.

In June 2013, I was sitting in the Detroit airport departure lounge, waiting for the plane that would take me on the third leg of my flight back to my home in San Antonio, Texas. Shortly after I'd found a seat in the crowded departure lounge, I watched a young woman in a wheelchair being pushed into the lounge by an airport porter. She gingerly stepped from the wheelchair to the adjacent seating, and as she did, she flashed a stunning smile in my direction. I looked behind me to see whom she might be smiling at, but there was no one in particular; it seemed that she was smiling for everyone in the lounge. I returned to reading my book and couldn't help overhear her making a reassuring phone call to what sounded like a small child. When the boarding of the flight was announced, I was one of the first down the jetway. I quickly found my window seat and returned to my book with my don't-even-try-to-talk-to-me earbuds firmly planted in my ears. A young woman engrossed in her own book occupied the aisle seat in the three-across row. Just before the doors of the half-filled flight were closed, the beautiful woman with the beckoning smile arrived at our row and pointed to the middle seat. She squeezed into the seat with a large carry-on bag and gifted me with another big smile. I smiled back but kept my head buried in my book.

When the flight attendant asked for our attention for the safety briefing, I took my earbuds out, and immediately, the young woman looked at me and asked about the ruby ring that I was wearing, a ring that I had been given forty-six years before by my late wife, Lindee. Looking at the ring, she said that her son had also given her a ruby ring, and then she stuck out her hand and said, "Hi, I'm Melissa!"

During the course of the three-hour flight, Melissa and I shared our stories. Mine was of losing my beloved wife just three years before, and hers was of the five-year battle she had been waging to stay alive after a near-fatal illness during her pregnancy and the subsequent severe damage it had done to all her vital organs, including her brainstem and heart. She looked strong and healthy, like the beauty queen she was, but on her left wrist, she wore an identification band from the hospital she had just left that belied her outward appearance. She was fighting to live, fighting for each new day with her four-year-old son Jack. Melissa and I talked about our lives throughout that journey, as it seems only strangers can on a long night flight. When we landed in San Antonio, I told her I would pray for her, and she responded that she'd be praying for me too. We said farewell as an airport porter arrived with a wheelchair to take her to meet her childhood friend waiting for her in the San Antonio terminal.

God's plan for our friendship didn't stop with that airport farewell. Throughout that summer, as Melissa often lay alone for days in her hospital bed, we would talk for hours by phone, and our friendship grew. Over the next year and a half, we would have periods of intense conversations and periods of quiet. I hadn't spoken to her in a few weeks when in October 2014 I was again sitting reading a book in another airport departure lounge, this time in Minneapolis. I glanced up from my book and saw a striking young woman with a very distinctive hairstyle entering the small newsstand near my flight gate. I had only seen that style once before, in a recent photo Melissa had posted on Facebook. I jumped from my seat and weaved my way through the crowd and tentatively said, "Melissa?" I was bald now from a recent round of chemotherapy, but Melissa turned and immediately recognized me from my voice. It was our first face-to-face encounter since that first plane ride. When we compared our tickets, we were delighted to discover we were again on the same flight and only one row apart. Our seat companions agreed to switch seats, and we shared another three hours of joyful conversation. We both agreed that our first plane ride might have been a coincidence, but the second one must have certainly been divinely orchestrated.

In the past six years, we have spent less than eight hours face-to-face, but we have shared hundreds of hours of conversations across the miles that separate us. In those conversations, I discovered in Melissa a consummate storyteller, and as she shared each chapter of her book, it became clear that she is also a talented writer. When she asked me to write this foreword, I was stunned. Why would she want me to write the foreword when she is a friend to celebrities, TV personalities, and a president? Any of them would be pleased to introduce Melissa and her book to the world. I'm unknown, except to her. My name and endorsement won't sell her book. But choosing me speaks to Melissa's character. She is a friend, and she does things her way, not the expected way. She is anything but predictable. She has never let poverty, illness, tragedy, or even her own fame distract her from her chosen path. And that is the Melissa I want to introduce to the reader, a determined mother who has written this book for a singular purpose—to be a legacy for her beloved son, Jack.

A year ago, before she began writing this book, Melissa was faced with yet another major medical crisis. The new illness would probably end her life in a year. The only hope was a surgical intervention that would be extremely painful and very likely could prove fatal due to her severely compromised physical condition. We often talked about her choices, and when she chose to go forward with the surgery, she told me, "I don't know how to give up. I don't know how to stop fighting." Once again, she was right about her decision to take on that battle, because, at her core, she is a fighter whose spirit is sourced by the solid ground of her faith, where fear has no foundation.

It is my privilege to invite each reader to participate in this legacy for Jack and share in Melissa's incredible story. You will laugh, you will cry, and often it will be hard to believe what you are reading. This is a story of the power of faith and forgiveness, perseverance against all odds, determination to fulfill a dream despite seemingly insurmountable challenges, uncanny physical strength, and a mother's fierce devotion to her son. In her book, Melissa has also charted a path for each of us to examine our own questions of character, like those that coursed through my mind during our first flight together.

What are *you* willing to fight for?

Gary D. Larsen, PhD
Colonel, USAF (Ret.)
San Antonio, Texas

Chapter 1

THE "THANK YOU" HEARD AROUND THE WORLD

Presidential candidate Donald J. Trump said, "We're going to be watching your boy . . . Something beautiful is going to happen. You watch." Those powerful words spoken to me at a campaign rally in Janesville, Wisconsin, forever changed the trajectory of my life. It was a moment that could only have been guided by the Divine. The day before, while lying in a hospital bed hooked up to IVs and tubes for oxygen, hydration, and nutrition, I could not possibly imagine what was to unfold. As a wife and mother battling an incurable illness, I never would have been okay leaving this earth without expressing my immense gratitude for the loving-kindness he had shown me and my sweet boy, Jack. This was personal—not political. And unbeknownst to me, the world was watching.

A hospital room was my second home back then, as it still is today and has been for more than a decade. I have a terminal condition called autonomic failure. As a child, I survived unimaginable traumas, including homelessness, and defying all odds, went on to be crowned Miss Wisconsin USA 2005. However, those challenges paled in comparison to the weight of the medical prognosis I was given in 2008 in conjunction with the birth of my son. There is much more to share about that in the pages ahead, but to say my health is severely compromised is an understatement.

In March 2016, while in a hospital in northeastern Wisconsin, I saw on the news that Donald Trump would be campaigning a few days later in Janesville, about three hours away. I cannot explain the feeling that came over me, but I knew I had to be there. It may sound irrational or dramatic to some, but to me, it meant everything. It was a one-in-a-million chance to thank the man who was the brightest light in the darkest time of my life.

Less than a year prior, I had written Mr. Trump to convey my deepest appreciation to him for a handwritten letter of encouragement he sent to me in 2014 at a time when, quite literally, my death was imminent and I had received last rites. The letter brought to my hospital room with explicit instructions that it be delivered by 8:00 a.m. ignited a fire in me when I had lost all hope. This man, whom I deeply admired and who was the measure of success in my eyes, gave me the will to keep fighting. His letter came at just the right time when those words were so desperately needed. I believed then, as I do now, that he saved me.

I never knew if he received my letter of gratitude, and I wondered about it often. So despite the serious medical risk I would be taking, I was determined to attend that rally. I submitted an online request for tickets and, the next day, received confirmation that my request was approved. My dear friend Deb, whose parents lived in Janesville, agreed to be my driver. In the chapters to come, you will hear more about this incredible woman's role in my life.

On the morning of the rally, March 29, 2016, I checked myself out of the hospital. By unhooking from the tubes and life-saving medical apparatus, I knew I was putting my life in jeopardy. On my wrist was a "do not resuscitate" bracelet. Fueled by sheer determination, Deb and I set off for Janesville.

Due to my illness, maintaining adequate blood pressure is difficult. As the miles sped by, I constantly adjusted my seat position to improve blood flow and avoid passing out, even lying down at times on a seat that had been folded flat.

I remember how bright the sun was that morning and how it warmed me through the car window as we drove. I felt peaceful, almost as if I was being led by the hand of God. I wore pajamas for warmth and comfort during the long drive, and when we arrived at the house of Deb's parents, I changed into an outfit my husband had brought to the hospital the night before. Then Deb, her sister, her father, and I headed to the rally while I silently prayed that I would get my chance to talk to Mr. Trump.

As we neared the event venue, a hotel and conference center, there were supporters and protesters everywhere. The large crowd was congregated mainly in the area closest to the exterior doors that led to the conference room where the rally would be held. Inching through the traffic, Deb snaked her way toward the lobby entrance of the hotel, intending to drop me off with her elderly father, who uses a walker. There were agents from the Secret Service near the entrance, and one of them rushed up to the van window, telling Deb to move the vehicle.

She explained that I was gravely ill and would not be able to walk the long distance from the parking area, and asked if we could wait there while she went to park. I mentioned that I was a former Miss Wisconsin USA and that Mr. Trump, who had owned the Miss Universe Organization (which also operates the Miss USA and Miss Teen USA pageants), had been so kind to me and that I was hoping for a chance to thank him at the rally. With my illness, you cannot tell from the outside how sick I am, although the agent could see that I was struggling to remain steady on my feet once I exited the van. He escorted Deb's father and me to the lobby to wait for Deb and her sister to return, and then the four of us remained there until the rally was ready to begin.

The agent came back to check on us a short while later, asking if I could sing—presumably since I had been in a pageant. Sing? He wanted me to sing the national anthem! I reluctantly told him no, not unless he wanted to see everyone cover their ears or leave Mr. Trump alone in an empty room. I was pretty desperate to see Mr. Trump, so I momentarily thought about saying yes. Trust me—singing the anthem would have been a disaster. That would have gone viral in a totally different way!

When it was time to move to the room where the rally would be held, the agent helped us make our way closer to the front row out of concern for my health and not wanting anyone to trip on the walker of Deb's father. By this time, I was feeling wiped out and dehydrated without the IV fluids I had been receiving in the hospital. A kind veteran and Trump supporter named Randal took notice of my struggles and offered me some water and a prayer for strength. I was so moved by his generosity. I happily accepted with a grateful heart.

While everyone was waiting for Mr. Trump to appear, I looked to the right of the stage and made eye contact with Tana Goertz, a woman I immediately recognized from season three of *The Apprentice*, Donald Trump's reality television program. That season was particularly memorable to me as it aired during my reign as Miss Wisconsin.

Tana, who later said that she had followed an inner voice, was holding a microphone and made her way over to me. I quickly learned that she was now the senior advisor and spokesperson for the Donald J. Trump Presidential Campaign. There was an instant connection. We talked briefly, and I told her what it would mean to me to convey my thanks to Mr. Trump. She said he wasn't taking any questions from the audience, but she would do her best to see if she could somehow help me.

When Mr. Trump took the stage, I cheered as loudly as I could, but my blood sugar was dropping, and I felt like I might pass out. I tried to catch his eye as I mouthed the words "thank you" while he smiled and waved at the crowd. It had been eleven years since we had met at the Miss USA pageant. My long hair was gone, a casualty of my illness, and I was surely unrecognizable as the woman he had met on a pageant stage over a decade ago.

About forty-five minutes into the rally, Tana took a risk and followed her heart. When an unexpected window of opportunity opened, she called out to him—her boss, the man who had made it clear that there were to be no questions—and said, "Mr. Trump, Melissa wants to thank you. She's got something to say."

The room, which just seconds before had been loud with cheers and excited banter, became eerily quiet as I took that microphone from Tana. You could hear a pin drop when I started to speak. My trembling voice was weak. I was overcome with emotion, and for the next few minutes, time stood still.

"I was Miss Wisconsin USA in 2005. I just want to say thank you. You saved me in so many ways. I have been struggling with an incurable illness, and I'm on home care now. It was caused by a doctor's medical negligence. In those dark days, fighting—right now all the tubes have been removed, and I have a "do not resuscitate" order—in those days in the hospital, I received from you a handwritten letter that said to the bravest woman I know.

"I'm here right now to thank you in person, and that was my biggest dream, to thank you, because through you and your organizations, my son, who is Mexican American, seven years old ... Just being able to stand on that stage with you back in 2005, the outpouring of love that came from that ultimately provided my son when he graduates high school with a full ride to college because of you. Your efforts have sent him to college. I've been writing letters to him for when I'm in heaven to tell him what you've done for him. Now he has a great responsibility to pay it forward just as you have done for us. I can't thank you enough."

Caught up in the moment, he came over to hug me and kissed my cheek as the crowd came alive again in an eruption of applause. He whispered, "Those doctors, they're going to be so wrong." Just then, I looked down and realized the necklace I was wearing had wrapped around the button of his suit coat. Secret Service agents started to move toward us because he couldn't pull away from me, not realizing we were stuck because of the necklace. I was able to unwrap it, but still, it was hard to let go. I had been so afraid that he would never understand what his kindness had meant to me and how it would change my son's life. But now that I had told him, I was at peace.

The significance of Tana handing me that microphone is astounding. To those in the room and those who have since seen the video clip from that rally, it should be evident by his initial body language and facial expression that Mr. Trump was clearly caught off guard. He took a couple of steps back as if bracing himself for the worst. He must have been extremely apprehensive, wondering who I was and what was going to come out of my mouth. Once he heard me speak, however, and remembered who I was, we shared the most unexpected, raw, and genuine of moments.

"There was nothing so beautiful as what she did. It's the most beautiful moment I have had since campaigning for president." Donald J. Trump

I truly believe God's handprints were all over that day. Tana's role, without a doubt, was not a coincidence but what I like to call a "God-incidence." Because of her bravery, my dying wish was granted. I have come to know her well in the years that followed.

She is a selfless giver, someone who isn't about position or title. The rally in Janesville was just the beginning of my relationship with Tana, the woman I consider a sister for life.

When Mr. Trump made his way back to the stage, people were visibly shaken by what they had witnessed. He looked at the crowd and said, "Wow. What a great woman that is—a great woman, a great mother . . . Something beautiful is going to happen. You watch." He seemed so moved by my words and told the crowd he was considering ending the rally on that note, saying, "I'd almost like to leave it there. We can't top that." Minutes later, he exited the stage as the up-tempo music signaled the end of the rally.

While making our way out of the building, several reporters with cameras stopped to ask my name, saying they were with this news channel or that one, but I could barely hear them above the noise of the crowd. At the time, it didn't seem like a big deal. Never did it occur to me while I was speaking to Mr. Trump or when I first settled in for the long drive back to the hospital that my "thank you" would be heard around the world. I had done what I set out to do, believing those few moments were seemingly between him, me, and the people witnessing it in the rally room that day. I thought I'd never see him again.

Afterward, I had no memory of the actual words I had spoken. It wasn't until I watched the playback of the rally that I realized it was the first time I had said in public that my illness was caused by a doctor's negligence. I had held it in for so many years, living in fear, because I was still under that medical facility's care. But now I had found my voice. I was finally free.

I will never know what impact my public expression of gratitude had on the electorate during the Wisconsin primary election and later during the presidential race. What I do know is that it came at a crucial time in Mr. Trump's campaign when his alleged attitude toward women and minorities had been unceasingly maligned by his opponents and the media. There was no denying that it had a profound impact on my life, the magnitude of which would soon be revealed.

Chapter 2

You Just Went Viral

As I settled into Deb's van for the long drive back to the hospital from the rally, my heart felt tremendous peace. I had set out on this journey with sheer determination to thank Mr. Trump for blessing my life. I wanted to do it for my son, Jack, too. I wanted Jack to see that gratitude truly is a magnet for miracles, that whatever it takes, never forget to express to people how much they mean to you. There is so much beauty in that. If it takes you having to do an army crawl to get to them, then do it! If someone changed your life, if someone blessed your life, make sure you stand up for what is right and thank them. I also wanted Jack to understand that we must do this at all cost.

With many overwhelming thoughts racing through my mind, the drive seemed to be flying by. I reclined my seat and decided to rest my eyes. It couldn't have been more than an hour into the ride when my phone began ringing incessantly from numbers I didn't recognize. As I was trying to make sense of what was happening, a familiar call came through. It was my dear friend and the reigning Miss Wisconsin USA, Kate Redeker. Fearing something bad might have happened because of all the previous unknown calls, I immediately flipped open my phone. (Yes, you read that right, at that time, I owned a ten-year-old flip phone.) I nervously answered, "Hello?"

In a very excited voice, she yelled, "Melissa, YOU JUST WENT VIRAL!" Being technically challenged, I had no idea what the word "viral" meant. She went on to explain, "You just thanked Donald Trump, right?"

I said, "Yes, how did you know?"

She then explained, "The video is trending online with over a million views."

What I thought was a private moment between Mr. Trump, myself, and the rally attendees was now being seen all over the world.

I returned to my hospital bed, once again receiving much-needed oxygen and IV hydration. I was still getting many calls from unfamiliar area codes. I never turn off my phone when I'm in the hospital away from my son just in case he needs me. It was obvious I wouldn't be getting any sleep that night, so I finally decided to take the next unknown call. It was a woman calling on behalf of Greta Van Susteren. She said, "Hello, Melissa. Will you do our show tomorrow?" I explained that I was getting many calls and didn't know what to do. She asked if I would give her my word that I would do her show first. Greta is a fellow Wisconsinite. She grew up just fifteen minutes from my hometown. One of my physicians, the one I like so much, graduated high school with her. Although we hadn't met, she felt familiar, like I knew her, so I gave her my word and agreed to do it. But there was a problem—I was back in the hospital and couldn't get to a studio. She said not to worry; they would do the show the next day live via Skype from my hospital bed.

My friend Deb set up her tablet on the hospital tray in front of me. I was in my pajamas, and you could hear the sound of my IV beeping in the background. It was my first time on live TV since 2005 when I competed in the Miss USA pageant. A lot had changed since then, from having long flowing hair and wearing a stunning evening gown to a hospital bed, in my pajamas, with tubes everywhere. Visually, I looked different, but my spirit burned brighter than ever before.

The next morning, I was scheduled to do my first live in-studio interview with Stuart Varney. The most beautiful black limousine picked me up from the hospital and drove me to the nearest FOX News studio in Green Bay, Wisconsin. Because I finally had a working IV in my arm and didn't want to risk losing the one good vein they could find, I kept the catheter in place and carried a fifteen-pound backpack that held my IV fluids along with a pump. Once I settled in at the anchor's desk for my live hit, the cameraman reassured me that they would only be filming from my elbows up. I was able to hide my tubes and backpack under the desk and at my feet. Just a few moments later, in my ear piece, I heard the warmest British accent: "Hi, Melissa. Can you hear me?" The heat from the studio lights and the echo of my own voice seemed to fade into the background. I instantly felt like I was talking with an old friend. I was blessed to be invited over half a dozen times on Stuart Varney's live television show, more than any other.

Days later, on April 3, 2016, after being interviewed on numerous other national news shows, Greta invited my family and me to attend a live town-hall taping with presidential candidate Donald J. Trump in Milwaukee, Wisconsin. Greta was so warm and kind when we arrived. She had a little green room set up for Jack next to her and her husband. Jack loved meeting her. You could see the joy on his face when they were introduced.

They started taping, and Jack would clap his little heart out at every commercial break. He was the only child in the audience and was so excited, proudly wearing his Trump hat and holding up his handmade sign that read: "Mr. Trump is my superhero."

After the live taping, Mr. Trump made his way over to us and reached his hands out to lift Jack and me onto the stage. That was the first meeting between Jack and the presidential candidate. Jack was in awe of the great man who had blessed our lives. Jack looked him in the eye and shook his hand with intention and said, "Nice to meet you Mr. President, sir." Mr. Trump responded with "Wow, what a kid." The election was far off, and the debates hadn't happened yet, but Jack was already calling him Mr. President. Jack sees things as they are; there is no in between.

To him, he was shaking the hand of a president. Now imagine, if only the polls and mainstream media were as intuitive as my sweet seven-year-old.

Jack has always had an eye for fashion and was enamored with Mr. Trump's tie. I gasped when I glanced down and realized that Jack had managed to pull it out of his suit coat and flipped it over to get a better look at it. I was quickly relieved when Mr. Trump looked at me with a great, big, kindhearted smile of understanding. I love the photo of Jack and Mr. Trump's meeting. It's one of my favorite photos of all time.

On the next night, April 4, 2016, I was invited to a live taping of another town hall. This time it was for the Sean Hannity show from Milwaukee. My husband, Sergio, and son, Jack, had to return home for work and school; so my dear friend and former Miss USA 2005, Chelsea Cooley, had flown in from North Carolina to be with me. Because of my failing health, I would need assistance, and it wasn't safe for me to be alone. During the taping, I was seated on the stage directly behind Mr. Hannity. This was our first meeting, and unbeknownst to me at the time, he would go on to bless my life in more ways than one. He became a close confidant, someone I could trust sharing my health battles and fear of death with. Even with his busy schedule, he found time to check on my well-being and get updates from my nurses. He was always in my corner. Above all, his greatest gift to me came one evening in the form of a conversation while I was in the hospital, preparing to undergo a high-risk medical procedure. I explained to him that I struggled greatly with surrendering to rest. I don't know how to stop fighting. I came into this world swinging, and I never had the luxury of hanging up my gloves. My physical body was so tired from battling an incurable illness for years, and I couldn't rest for fear that if I did, God would take me home. Mr. Hannity changed my life with this advice: "Melissa, it's okay to rest. Remember, no matter what you do, no matter how hard you fight, you cannot live one second past what God has written for you."

Those were the profound words I needed to hear for so long. I wasn't the one in control of my survival. My fate was in the hands of God Almighty. It was okay to rest in His loving arms. For the first time, I was able to exhale.

At the end of the show, Mr. Trump looked over at me with a warm smile and asked, "Are you going to the rally after this?"

I explained, "I don't have a ticket, and I don't think I can make it over there in time."

"Okay," he said, "you can come with us."

It was a freezing-cold early spring night in Wisconsin. Without our coats, we were quickly being whisked out a backdoor. The Secret Service was helping Mr. Trump and Melania out to the motorcade. For safety reasons, we had to keep moving and couldn't stop. At that moment, Mr. Trump looked over and noticed that I was shivering. He immediately went to remove the long black coat from his body to hand to Secret Service to put over me. He wasn't thinking of his safety at that moment; he was thinking of me in the cold. The future president of the United States literally stopped to give me the coat off his back.

I was riding in the motorcade, following Mr. Trump and Melania to the rally. As we were going through every red light, I was thinking back to my childhood, my little-girl self who was born into severe poverty—it was a surreal experience. I was trying to take in the moment for that little girl who was homeless and had big dreams of being somebody beyond the circumstances she was born into.

Once Chelsea and I arrived at the very loud, jam-packed venue, we were quickly escorted into a backroom where Mr. Trump and Melania were waiting. The regal couple was standing next to a table, looking down at an open laptop. All of a sudden, I heard my shaky voice. I realized Mr. Trump was showing Melania the video of me thanking him just days before. As I glanced at her stunningly beautiful face, I noticed tears welling up in her eyes—one mother watching another.

Moments later, Mr. Trump took the stage. I was watching in the wings when I heard him mention my name to his very large audience.

"There is a very special woman, an incredible woman, and Melania just said hello and met her, and she was so taken, and she represented you so beautifully. Many of you know who she is, but she was Miss Wisconsin. She has one of the most incredible spirits that I've ever seen. She has a husband and a son, and her son is absolutely magnificent, and she loves him more than anything you could imagine. She's going through a very hard time, and she has been so supportive and so incredible of what we are all trying to do, 'Make America great again,' and bring it back, and she is with a friend of hers who's very well known, Chelsea Cooley, who is such a great friend of Melissa Young. I'd like to bring her onto the stage, and maybe Melissa would like to say something. This is just an unbelievable woman, so could I ask Melissa to come out on stage, please?"

My heart sank into the pit of my stomach. I had nothing prepared, but then I thought about what Mr. Trump had just said: I am the mother of a magnificent son, and I want nothing more than for him to grow up in a country that is safe. I knew with Mr. Trump as our president, he would make that happen. With a gentle nudge from Chelsea, I walked out from behind the curtain and onto the stage.

There I was speaking to thousands of fellow Wisconsinites. As Mr. Trump later said, I spoke from my heart; there were no teleprompters.

When I finished, he put his arm around me and walked me back to Chelsea and Melania.

As he made his way back to the podium, the whole room erupted, chanting, "President Trump! President Trump! President Trump!" It was in that moment that the spirit of the large crowd lifted. They loved him, just like I did.

As Mr. Trump continued his speech, I sat backstage with Melania. She asked about Jack and shared about Barron. She gave me valuable, loving advice about what was to come in the next few years as her beloved son is two years older than mine. It had been a long day without my IV hydration and nutrition, and I started to not feel so well. Melania must have seen it written all over my face as she kindly held my hand and asked for security to get me a chair. Pastor Mark Burns was there with his lovely wife, Tomarra. He asked, "Can we say a prayer over you?" Pastor Burns then lifted me up with the most heartfelt prayer. I was so moved by this wonderful man of God and his loving-kindness.

A short time later, everything went dark. I passed out. I woke up to a team of EMTs standing over me, and when I looked at my side, there was Melania next to me, holding my hand. In the warmest, most compassionate, mother-like way, she whispered, "Melissa, you go to the hospital, and we'll see you again. Please go to the hospital. We need you to be okay."

The future first lady of the United States, with all her goodness and grace, was tending to me, caring for me, worrying about me more than what was happening on stage.

Chapter 3

Young Love

My maternal grandparents, Cliff and Nancy Kay, were sweethearts since their early teens. They shared a strong Catholic faith and a love for each other that was nothing short of a fairy tale. With movie-star looks, like Natalie Wood and James Dean, Cliff had piercing blues eyes and was handsome as a young man could be. Nancy Kay was a breathtaking brown-eyed beauty. They were born during the Great Depression. Cliff's family struggled like so many. As a child, he was the only one in his family to own a bicycle, a rare luxury during that time. His bike meant everything to him until he laid eyes on Nancy Kay. Cliff wasn't the only young man with eyes for the raven-haired beauty. His brother had them too. Worried he might lose his chance at winning her heart, Cliff offered his brother his most-prized possession to back away from Nancy Kay. Without that exchange, the lives of over one hundred people might not exist, including mine. Cliff and Nancy were married on June 10, 1953. They had ten children. My mother, Micky, was their fifth child born in the late 1950s.

Micky is my mother's nickname. It was given to her by her older brother Billy when my grandmother brought her home from the hospital. He called her Micky Mouse, and from that day forward, she was known as such. She had a happy early

childhood living in the country in a rented old farmhouse with
her many siblings. Her father, Cliff, was a hard worker and an
incredible handyman. He once built a shed at the end of their
very long driveway for her and her siblings to stay warm while
they waited for the school bus during the cold Wisconsin winters.
He and Nancy were fantastic ice skaters. He made a pond in the
back of their farmhouse. Every winter, they would put on ice-
skating shows for their children. They also loved to dance, and
when doing so, everyone in the room would take a seat to enjoy
but also to not be upstaged by the graceful couple.

Cliff and Nancy

After Micky finished third grade, her parents uprooted their
family and moved to the city. Nancy and Cliff were close friends
with another beautiful couple named Carol and Duane. Carol's
oldest son, Mike, was best friends with Micky's older brother Billy;
and from the fifth grade on, Micky and Mike were childhood

sweethearts. A few years later, Carol's beloved husband, Duane, was killed in a semi truck accident. He was thirty-eight years old. The tragic accident that took Duane's life affected the lives of many. Carol was left with five young children at home.

Duane

Mike was fifteen, the oldest, and now the man of the house. Mike often turned to Micky's father, Cliff, for advice; and he had no problem giving it, along with a kick in the butt at times. Nevertheless, Cliff and Nancy loved Mike as if he were their own son. Just like everybody else in town, they also saw a future between him and their daughter Micky.

When Mike turned eighteen, he joined the United States Navy. Micky was sixteen, going to school, and working two jobs. Mike was stationed in Virginia and traveled to the US Virgin Islands. He liked working in the kitchen on the large ship and was known for his outstanding cooking skills. His shipmates enjoyed his signature chili, a recipe that could have only come from a true Wisconsinite. Kitchen duties helped to pass the time, but nothing seemed to help the heartsick feeling of missing

Micky. In the silence of the night surrounded by blue water, with a US Navy bracelet inscribed "Micky" wrapped tightly around his thick wrist, Mike poured out his heart into love letters.

When Mike returned to solid ground on a naval base in Waukegan, Illinois, he was allowed one or two weekends a month to cross over into Wisconsin to visit his love, but it wasn't without conditions. Mike's naval officer often agreed to extend his visits in exchange for fresh Wisconsin cheese, a pretty nice deal for the two of them.

While Mike was stationed in Illinois, Micky met Tom at her second job cleaning offices. Tom was a self-assured gentleman ten years her senior. He lived thirty miles outside of town and owned hundreds of acres of land. Like many young men, Tom was smitten by Micky's wit and striking beauty. Tom confided to his buddy and coworker at the office: "I'm going to ask Micky on a date." His buddy laughed because Micky wasn't only considered beautiful but also considered taken. Tom confidently made a bet with his buddy: "If she says no, I'll give you forty acres of my land." Tom's confidence and charm worked. The naive young woman who grew up on a farm in the middle of nowhere and was in love with the same boy since the fifth grade agreed to go on a date with the older out-of-towner—a decision that would cause unintended consequences and affect her life forever.

Longing for more life experiences and opportunities beyond the small world in which she lived, Micky attempted to break through the bubble that had enveloped her and her family. Micky wanted more. After a few secret dates with Tom, she made the painful decision to write Mike, the only love she ever knew, a "Dear John" letter.

Upon reading the letter, Mike was shattered and couldn't bear the thought of losing Micky. It wasn't his weekend to be on leave, but in a panic, he made a plea to his naval officer and was ultimately granted permission.

Micky was getting ready for a date with Tom. This would be the first and only time he was going to pick her up at her parents' house. As Tom made his way to her front door, just before knocking, a loud muscle car pulled up. Mike jumped out of the car and walked up behind Tom. Just then, Micky opened the door, shocked to see the two men staring back at her. She asked Mike, "What are you doing here? You aren't supposed to be home. Didn't you get my letter?"

Mike poked his finger into Tom's chest and demanded, "Where do you think you're going with her?"

Tom said, "I'm taking her to see my farm."

Micky backed up as Mike barged into the house, waking up her parents, Cliff and Nancy.

Cliff yelled, "What's going on out there?"

Mike turned back toward the door, rushing past Micky and Tom, and back to his car. Micky, who still loved Mike, hurried after him. Mike slammed the car door, fired up the engine, and squealed out. He sped down the road at a dangerous speed. Seconds later, in a cloud of smoke, a loud metallic bang that could be heard from miles away pierced their ears and shook Micky to her core. She could see the horrific accident. Mike had wrapped his Gran Torino around a tree. Micky screamed and raced to the scene as fast as her legs could carry her. The driver side door was horseshoed around a large white oak tree. When the paramedics arrived, they helped pull Mike's broken body through the windshield in what was left of the car.

By the grace of God, Mike's life was spared on that late summer night. He suffered a serious neck injury and was discharged from the US Navy.

Micky blamed herself for the accident, and so did everyone else. She was riddled with guilt and immediately stopped seeing Tom. A month later, Micky was called into the kitchen for a family meeting. Present were her parents, Cliff and Nancy, her older brother Billy, and Mike's mother, Carol.

Micky knew exactly what was up. She had been feeling the pressure to make a commitment to Mike. She loved him dearly but longed for a life outside of her own backyard. With all eyes on her, in a firm voice, Cliff told her to sit down. "What are you going to do?" he asked. "Are you going to marry him or not?"

She softly replied, "Yeah."

Cliff picked up the phone on the wall behind him and turned the numbered disk. He uttered into the headset, "She said yes."

Three days later, on August 3, 1974, my parents, Michael Duane Young (nineteen) and Micky Faucher (seventeen) were married in a small ceremony.

Some people are destined to fall in love with each other . . . but not destined to stay together.

Chapter 4

FOREVER IN BLUE JEANS

My parents, Mike and Micky, were newlyweds and just kids themselves when they started a family of their own. Their first child, my sister Michelle, was born on April 1, 1975. My brother Michael Jr. soon followed on November 5, 1977. Times were hard for the young couple. They moved from a camper to a small apartment a few miles outside of their hometown. Mike was on the road a lot, making a small living driving a semi truck. Micky taught Sunday school at their church. She was also expecting again.

It was early springtime, and Micky was nine months along. She decided to join Mike on an overnight haul. Their kind neighbor agreed to watch Michelle and Michael Jr. With a bed in the back of the semi and her doctor's permission, Mike and Micky hit the road for what they thought would be a nice little break before baby number 3.

After driving all day across the state of Wisconsin, Mike and Micky pulled over on a Native American reservation for a good night's sleep, something Micky wasn't used to with two babies at home and financial worries weighing heavily on her mind.

The next morning, it was hard to tell that the sun came up. It was dark and storming. They decided to wait for the bad weather to subside before heading home. Around 11:00 a.m. Micky ran through the harsh downpour to wash up in the truck stop located near where they had slept. In the truck stop, she took a shower and put on a fresh T-shirt and worn-out blue jeans. Micky was too small for maternity clothes and could still fit into her everyday outfits.

Shielding herself from the whipping wind and rain, she darted across the road and back to the semi truck. She hopped into the seat next to Mike, and when she looked down at her blue jeans, she noticed she was sitting in a puddle of water. She immediately discovered the puddle wasn't from the rain; her water had broken.

Mike ran as fast as his muscular legs could go. He pushed opened the door to the truck stop and yelled, "My wife is in labor! Where is the nearest hospital?"

The man behind the counter said, "It's five miles north but—"

The man never had an opportunity to finish what he was saying. The door had already closed behind Mike, and he was halfway across the road, making his way back to Micky. Mike drove the semi-truck through the terrible storm until they arrived at the nearest medical facility. They were in the middle of nowhere, and what the man at the truck stop had called a "hospital" was, in fact, a tiny clinic where they saw patients for fevers and minor cuts and bumps. At this point, it didn't matter; their baby was coming.

The soaking-wet couple was greeted by a sweet lady behind the front desk. "How may I help you?" she asked.

Micky explained, "I'm in labor."

The lady peeked over her desk and looked Micky up and down. "That's impossible!" the lady shouted. Then she hurried down the hall to get the only doctor there.

He took one look at Micky and said, "No way is this woman ready to have that baby."

Mike insisted, "She's nine months pregnant, and her water broke!"

The small staff scrambled around, gathering everything they thought was needed. The clinic only had four beds, none of which were intended for childbirth. The Band-Aid doctor glanced at Mike, who was standing outside the room, a familiar place for him to wait. He hadn't seen the birth of their other two children.

The doctor reached out and pulled Mike into the room by his collar. "Get in here, we're in this together!" he demanded. Mike's face was as white as the bed sheets while he held Micky's hand.

A few moments later, at 1:18 p.m., a faint cry from their baby girl brought tears to everyone's eyes. Micky's first words were "She's so tiny."

The doctor looked at Mike and asked, "Are you going to be all right?"

He said, "Yes," with tears in his eyes.

I was born on May 9, 1979, weighing two pounds, thirteen ounces. My little brother Mitchell arrived thirteen months later.

I came into this world a fighter and would never get to take my gloves off.

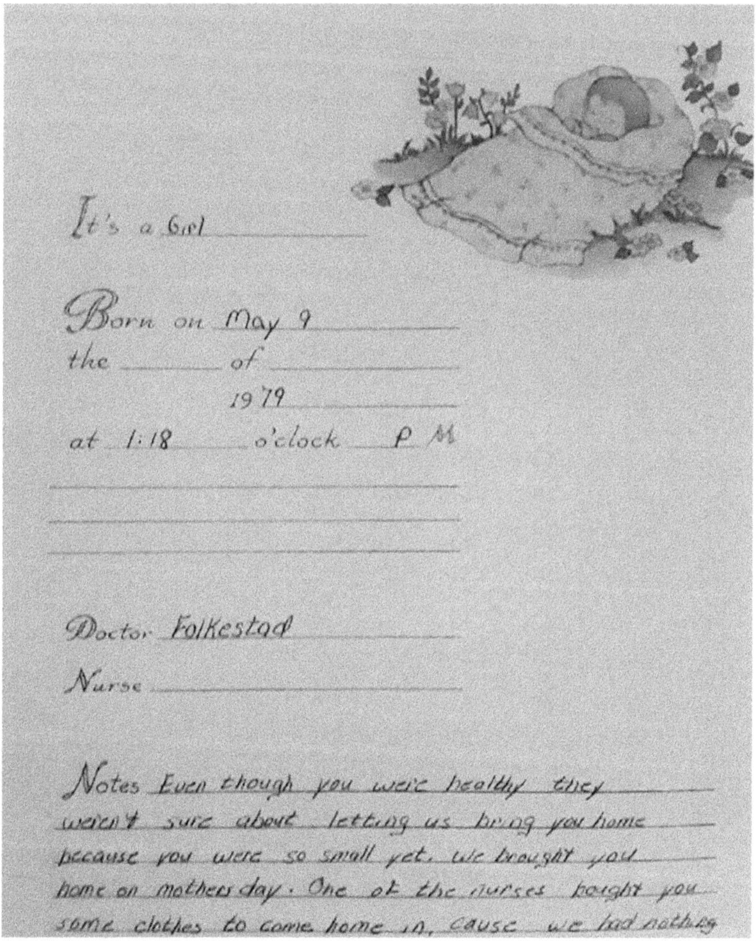

It's a Girl

Born on May 9
the _____ of _____
19 79
at 1:18 o'clock P M
_____
_____
_____

Doctor Folkestad

Nurse _____

Notes Even though you were healthy they weren't sure about letting us bring you home because you were so small yet. We brought you home on mothers day. One of the nurses bought you some clothes to come home in, cause we had nothing

The President was Carter

Popular Entertainers Andy Gibb

Fashions and Fads

The most popular Song (Daddys Favorite) Music box dance - (moms Favorite) Forever in Bluejeans

The most popular Dance Disco

Health Examinations

The first after birth   Date 9-16-79

you were so small one
of the other doctors came
out and saw you Also. she
pasted you around to all the
other nurses saying - just
hold her once she's just
like a baby puppy. the
reason for the visit was
to see if you needed to
go back into a nursery now
that we were back home.
Dr. Wallace said everything seemed
fine. you may be a week or 2
early. but you seemed healthy

Chapter 5

I Am Weak, but He Is Strong

Only six photos, total, exist of me from birth through childhood. Here are two of them taken at ages three and five. I only owned one dress; as you can see, I am wearing it in both photos. It was handed down to me from a woman at church after her daughter grew out of it.

Aside from that dress, I wore my older brother Michael's hand-me-downs. Michael was very active and always on the move. His clothes were handed down to him from family and fellow church members, so by the time they were passed on to me, they were grass-stained and worn. Along with Michael's hand-me-downs, I shared a pair of torn brown shoes with my little brother Mitchell. I was so thankful that school photos didn't show my feet. In my heart, I loved all thing princess and girly, but I didn't have the option to wear anything that would make me feel that way.

I was a very observant little girl, always studying people and my surroundings; but I was also painfully shy, which made me key into situations even more so. My first teacher once wrote in her notes that I was "afraid to blink." She wasn't exaggerating. The only time I felt like I could come out of my shell was with my siblings. Together, I was the silly one that was always cracking jokes and pulling pranks. But in public, I was silent and dreaded when anyone looked my way.

I was the smallest student in my kindergarten class, measuring at the ninth percentile for my height and weight. The seating chart was in alphabetical order, so with the last name Young, my desk was in the back of the classroom. There was a bench underneath my desk to prevent my feet from dangling all day and a dictionary on my seat so I could see the teacher. I loved sitting in the back because I didn't feel like anyone was looking at me, and then I could daydream and talk to Jesus. I had countless conversations with Him in that back corner. I also loved to observe.

I would look at the other girls in their pretty dresses, tights, and shiny shoes. I remember how the little girl who sat next to me always smelled so clean. I imagined her soap was pink, like flowers. Her hair was perfect, her dresses had ruffles, and her bright white tights complimented her polished saddle shoes. The girls in my class always looked so beautiful to me. I never felt jealous though; they gave me something to dream about. I would escape into their world; I could forget for a moment that I was hungry or that I had to wash up in public restrooms before school because there was no hot water and electricity at my home. I was just the little girl in the back row, wearing boy's clothes, who secretly dreamed of being a princess.

As much as I feared being noticed in the classroom, it didn't compare to the anxiety and embarrassment that came at lunchtime. The other kids had metal lunch boxes with little thermoses that always seemed to have something warm to eat inside. On most days, during lunch, I had nothing to open and nothing to eat. I used every trick I could think of to avoid sitting in the cafeteria. I'd hide behind a bathroom stall or conveniently get a bellyache and visit the nurse, anything to fill the gap between lunch and recess.

Recess was my favorite thing about school. Every afternoon, I ran directly to the swings on the playground. I would look up at the sky and point my toes to heaven. "Please, Jesus, turn these old boy shoes into shiny girl ones," I'd whisper. I believed that if I could just swing high enough, He would slip them on my feet. Swinging also gave me another opportunity to daydream about a different life, the one I had created in my imagination. Being a dreamer carried me through tough times and preserved my innocence. If I wasn't a dreamer, I would have had to face my reality, and I believe it would have hardened my soft heart.

At home, I felt loved by my parents and three siblings, but I also felt the stress of our struggles. I was a daddy's girl but followed my busy mom everywhere I could. Everyone called me "Micky's little shadow." Like a safety blanket, I held on to her for dear life. My older sister Michelle was my protector. My oldest brother Michael was sensitive underneath but always bouncing off the walls to deflect. My little brother Mitchell was my sidekick and happily agreed to do anything I'd ask. It's safe to say that Mitchell and I were the closest, being just thirteen months apart. We had our own language that no one could understand but us. I was sad leaving him to go to school but was thankful to get to wear the shoes we both shared.

The mile-long walk to school seemed so far for my tiny legs to take me. The journey was even more difficult for my siblings and me during Wisconsin's bitter-cold winters. The temperature would drop into the single digits, cold enough to freeze over a nearby lake. To walk through the woods, which was covered in deep, deep snow would take longer. So as a shortcut, we would walk across the frozen lake.

One bitter-cold winter morning, on my way to school, I was trailing behind, carrying my rented library books and school papers. I was crying; it hurt to walk in the cold because I didn't have the proper winter clothing. My eyelashes had frozen droplets of tears on them and were sticking together. To cope with the brutal journey, I did what I knew best—I started daydreaming. I was imagining I was a beautiful princess gracefully gliding across the frozen lake to get to my castle. Suddenly, I was shocked back to reality by the frigid-cold water. While daydreaming, my right leg had fallen through an ice fisherman's hole. My leg was submerged past my knee. I dropped everything I was carrying and grabbed at the solid ice around me. What I had been crying about just moments earlier actually was a blessing in disguise. Having no mittens on my hands allowed me to scratch and claw at the ice, preventing my tiny body from completely slipping through the fisherman's hole and into the deep lake. In that moment of sheer panic, I felt something underneath my foot. Whatever it was, it gave me a helpful boost. What was difficult was now easy. I just pulled my leg up and out of the hole. I looked down, and the shoe that didn't fit properly was no longer on my foot. There I was sitting in the middle of an icy lake with a soaking wet pant leg and sock. I still had quite a long journey to school, and for some reason, I never thought about turning around and going back home. I guess I knew that wasn't going to change anything; there wasn't anybody who could fix it for me.

Even at that young age, I knew I had to keep pressing on and moving forward. Always a problem solver, I picked up my books and papers and continued my journey across the lake. I carried my things in one hand and used the other to hold up my wet sock and pull it from sticking to the ice. My wet pant leg immediately began to freeze, which made it difficult to bend my knee with each step. To prevent myself from crying, I began to sing, "Yes, Jesus loves me. Yes, Jesus loves me. Oh yes, Jesus loves me, for the Bible tells me so."

I finally arrived at school, pried open the large door, and immediately noticed the empty hallway. It hit me—I was late, and the students were already seated at their desks. I was afraid that I would have to walk in front of my class wearing only one shoe and frozen pants. As I made my way down the empty hallway, I ran into a teacher who was standing on a stepladder, hanging our handmade Christmas ornaments. She glanced down at me and did a quick double-take. "Where is your shoe, young lady?" she asked in a firm voice.

"It's in the lake," I painfully replied. She pointed down the hall with an ornament dangling through her fingers.

"Go directly to the office," she demanded with a frown.

With my head down, I made my way into the office. The office lady sent me to see the school nurse. When the nurse removed my wet sock, my foot was a bluish-purple color. She warmed it with a heating pad and dry towel. I was praying that I could just stay hidden in her room for the rest of the day, but as soon as my foot turned pale pink, she guided me off the table and out into the hallway. I followed her to the lost-and-found where we dug for dry clothes. I was too tiny to fit into the articles of clothing that we pulled out. At the bottom of the bin was one left boot. She slipped it onto my right foot and said, "You'll have to make do." That wasn't the first time I had heard those words, and it certainly wouldn't be the last. "Making do" was all I knew.

I walked into my classroom, handed my teacher a late slip, and silently prayed, "Please, Jesus, don't let them look at my feet." He must have been busy that morning because He didn't hear my prayer. My classmates immediately started laughing at me. One boy shouted, "Melissa peed her pants." Another boy snickered, "And her boot is on the wrong foot." I quickly sat down at my desk and closed my eyes to disappear, and there in the back of the room, I talked to Jesus.

Recently, I was asked what advice I would give my younger self. Well, I'd tell this little girl not to be so timid and afraid. Trust in God; His plan for your life is breathtaking. Follow your heart; gratitude will take you to places beyond your dreams. Keep the faith; your day in the sun will come, and it will shine upon you in more beautiful ways than you can imagine because one thing I know for sure is that light shines brightest in the darkness.

Chapter 6

God's House

Winter had passed, but our struggles had not. My parents were knee-deep in overdue bills, and the wolf was constantly at the door. My father was working for pennies at a salvage yard, and my mother was doing everything she could to care for the four of us without the proper means to do so. As exhausted as she was, she still managed to give back, volunteering at church, putting care packages together to send overseas, while at the same time, not knowing how she was going to provide those same things for her own children

My parents were doing their best, but it wasn't enough. They were kids raising kids. From the very beginning, Mike and Micky's childhood romance was destined to disintegrate under the pressure of real-life hardships. A financial situation so dire with no intervention would ultimately lead to the breakdown of our family. The young couple that never fell out of love but simply fell out of resources sadly went their separate ways.

My mother came from a very large family; she was the middle child of ten. Her older siblings were having families and were struggling too. To take the four of us in wasn't something they could do. Some were living in trailers, some in small apartments that couldn't accommodate more children. It was too much for them. It wasn't like we just needed a place to stay for the weekend; we needed life-changing help—we needed a home. My grandparents, Cliff and Nancy, were still raising my mother's younger siblings. It was an overwhelming situation for everybody, and they didn't have much to offer. The four of us were loved by our family, but the financial resources were just not there.

With no utilities for months, our landlord hand-delivered an eviction notice to my now-single mother, along with an unwelcome proposition. The greasy-haired, overweight, unkempt man offered to overlook some of the debt in exchange for her company. In what I can only imagine was her most desperate hour, she kept her dignity, turned down the devil, and took her troubles to God.

Feeling hopeless, my mother, who was a Sunday school teacher, knew that she had to find help from our place of worship. She dressed us up in our best hand-me-downs and walked us to our church—what I as a child called God's house.

We sat up straight in the old church pews, not understanding what we were doing there on a weekday. We listened intently as our mother begged for help from our priest, telling him the desperate circumstances we were facing. This was the first time I had ever seen my mother cry. As she humbly asked for help from the church she had served since her childhood, our priest prayed with us, then excused himself and never returned. We sat quietly in the chapel, waiting for what seemed like an eternity, when finally the church secretary, who knew our family well, appeared with something large in her arms. When she approached us, she spoke no words and made no eye contact. She then handed my mother the large object.

We walked out of the church, single file behind our mother. She had us sit next to her on the front steps and explained that we were worth more than this, referring to the awkward object she was now holding. She said through her tears, "Do not let this define you." I soon learned that what my mother was holding was a tent and our new home.

Chapter 7

THE TENT THAT SHAPED ME

My mother told us we were worth more than the tent given to us by our church, but I didn't feel that way. I was the little girl who spent most of my time daydreaming and talking to Jesus. Who was I talking to exactly, and where was He? "I need You, Jesus," I'd cry out. "I'll be the best little girl in the world," I promised. I wish somebody would have told me then that Jesus doesn't make deals like that. His blessings aren't contingent on our good or bad behaviors. His plan is purposeful, and it's during our hardships that He is most present.

After our eviction, my mother took us to stay with our wonderful neighbor lady, Ms. Lederhaus. She was a single mother raising two young boys, a little bit older than me. She never had a daughter and would watch us from time to time. She always paid special attention to me. As a middle child, I loved her attention. I also loved her very much. We stayed with her and her boys for a short time. She was struggling as well, and four additional children were way beyond her means. My father wasn't present during this time. I believe he was living with a friend somewhere.

With all resources exhausted, what little resources she had, my mother packed up our small rundown truck that only had a bench seat. My three siblings sat on the seat, and I sat on the floor because I was the smallest. It was impossible for us to live in the truck, so she drove us to a park in the country.

My mother set up the tent at Huckleberry Park in what looked like a camping area. That was our new home; that's where we lived. We would all squeeze into the truck if it was raining or if the weather was bad. I remember one night there was a violent thunderstorm; the five of us piled into the old truck and slept on top of one another. Otherwise, we stayed in the tent. Sometimes, we would get a box of snack cakes, with maybe six in a box. That's what we would eat for dinner. It didn't go unnoticed by me that on most nights, my mother would get nothing to eat.

My little brother Mitchell (the one I share a special bond with and our own language) and I came up with what we thought was a clever way to silence the sounds of our growling bellies. After saying our nightly prayers and before lying our heads down to sleep in the tent, we made a pact that we would dream about Thanksgiving dinner. In the morning, we would share with each other all the wonderful foods we ate in our dreams. I always had a sweet tooth, so naturally, I told him about all the pies I enjoyed. Mitchell, who was always the first one at the table and the last one to leave, described his dreams of eating mounds of stuffing and mashed potatoes covered in gravy. Now, looking back, I don't think I ever had an actual dream about eating those warm pies; and I'm certain Mitchell never had dreams of stuffing and potatoes. We lied; we were simply two little kids comforting each other with dreams of a less-painful reality.

One afternoon, while Mitchell and I were playing in the park, I found a half-eaten candy necklace in the grass. I immediately picked it up against my brother's advice. "Sissa, that's gross!" he shouted. Even with my sweet tooth and an empty stomach, it wasn't candy to me. I had a vision in my head of what it could be. Instead, I saw a beautiful pearl necklace. With the string of candy around my neck, I made believe that I was Jackie Kennedy.

Being "Jackie Kennedy" with my candy pearls brought beauty and wonder to my days living in the park. When playing house with other kids, I was classy and married to Jack Kennedy. An older boy thought he'd burst my bubble by teasing me, "You can't be married to JFK. He's dead!" He repeated as he followed me around the park. His words didn't mean a thing to me. As far as I was concerned, my dirty-blonde hair was black, and my old hand-me-downs were stunning designer garments. All it took was a half-eaten candy necklace, and I was somebody special.

The sad thing about daydreams and candy necklaces is that they don't last forever. At the end of the day, I was forced to face reality. I was homeless and hungry, living in a tent. Despite what my mother had told us, I believed that's what God gave me because that's what He thought I was worth—a self-belief that I would carry for decades to come.

Little did I know then, one day, God would take me back to His old tent and show me that it was a priceless gift made of gold. He hadn't overlooked me after all.

Chapter 8

PLEASE DON'T TAKE MY SUNSHINE AWAY

I remember my mother once said, "All they have is each other." After living in a tent in the park, going to bed hungry, dreaming of my next meal, my beautiful mother became ill and was diagnosed with lymphoblastic leukemia. She was hospitalized and could no longer feed or care for my siblings and me. With a promise made by a social worker to my mother that they would keep the four of us together, she painfully agreed it was necessary to place us into foster care.

When the social worker picked us up, my ill mother insisted that she ride along. The social worker agreed. That drive is forever burned into my memory. I remember how my mother looked so heartbroken. I knew something was wrong. Since I was very little, I was always tuned in to other people's feelings and emotions. I would take them on as my own so I could feel my mother's sadness and heartache. No matter what she said, I knew better. For some reason, it felt like goodbye. Those words were never said, but it felt that way.

I remember holding on to her pant leg so tightly. I was always called "Micky's shadow" or "little Micky" because wherever she was, I was, and we looked just alike. Our bond was immeasurable.

When we pulled up to our new "home," I looked out of the car window and noticed the house of my mother's parents. My grandparents Cliff and Nancy lived just across the road. As we made our way to the front porch, I could still see it over my right shoulder. We were walking into strangers' home; this is where we were going to live now.

The social worker told me to let go of my mother, but I couldn't do it. I gripped her pant leg tighter as sheer terror took over my small body. My thoughts on the drive there were correct—something was wrong. The foster mother told us it was time for our mother to leave. "Please don't go! Please don't leave me, Mommy! I need you!" I screamed as the social worker pried each one of my fingers from my mother's pant leg. Tears were pouring down my face. My older sister Michelle, my protector, took me into her arms. We all huddled together as we watched our mother walk away and drive down the road and out of our sight. She was gone. Her favorite lullaby to sing to us since we were babies was "You Are My Sunshine." All I could think of at that moment was "Please, Jesus, don't take my sunshine away" because that's what she was to me. She was the sunshine, and now everything was gray.

The foster mother was making dinner, which should have been wonderful with all the amazing smells of a homemade meal, but instead, it felt overwhelming. Here was a table being set with all this food, but there wasn't warmth in the home; it was cold. She and her husband had two sons of their own. The man of the house had a very stern voice that was scary to me. I wasn't used to that; my father always spoke to us in a soft and gentle voice. This man had a very upset and unhappy-looking face. He scared me, so I clung to my older sister. If she walked to the couch, I walked to the couch. If she walked to the restroom, I followed. I now became her shadow.

The foster home had a long kitchen table with bench seats on each side, so we all sat together on a single bench. The foster mother put a huge plate of food in front of me, which made me feel even more overwhelmed. I was so heartbroken about being away from my mother that I couldn't eat. I'm sure I was hungry because I was watching my brothers scarf down their meals. My little brother was so hungry that he picked up the big bowl of applesauce. I remember him looking up at me with his bright-blue eyes through his hair. His long bangs were covered in applesauce because he had put his whole head in the bowl. He didn't want to leave one morsel behind, but I had no appetite.

The father of the home said in a very stern voice that I wasn't leaving the table until I finished all my food. The amount of food just looked like too much, and I knew that I couldn't eat it.

My sister begged me to please eat, so I tried, but I immediately started to gag. The foster mother firmly escorted me to the restroom, where I spit the food out into the toilet. She then told me to return to the table and finish eating. I started sobbing as I tried to take in another bite, but once again, I couldn't do it. Without warning, the man of the house lifted me up off the bench by my arm and started hitting me with everything he had over and over. My siblings started screaming. He saw that I was their weakness. They had tough faces when we walked in, but when it came to me, it broke them. They never had to protect me from an adult; we had never been mistreated or abused. We were so well behaved. I don't remember much discipline in our home with my parents, so this was horrific. My body was swinging back and forth like a rag doll with each strike. He seemed so big to me, and I was petrified.

That night, we were taken upstairs to our room in the attic. My battered body hurt with every move, but nothing was as painful as the heartbreak I felt. From the attic, through a tiny window, we could see our grandparents' house across the road. They were right there, yet for some reason, we couldn't get to them.

I spent many sunny days peering out of the attic window, staring at my grandparents' house. My grandfather Cliff, who was an amazing handyman, had built a swimming pool out of an old silo in their backyard. I would watch many of my cousins, most of them around our age, come and go with their swimsuits and inner tubes. At the same time, my brother Michael, who was just a year older than me, would be chopping wood in the backyard of where we were now living. He was the scrawniest little guy, and I could hear him swinging that ax all day long. I cannot imagine how tired he was.

From the very beginning, the foster father picked up on the fact that I was my siblings' weakness. For anything any of us did wrong, even if I had nothing to do with it, he would hurt me to punish them.

My spirit was shattered. I couldn't daydream my way out of this situation, and my usual conversations with Jesus had gone silent.

Eventually, our foster parents moved me from the room we all shared together in the attic to a tiny room by myself. I was the little girl who was afraid to blink in my everyday life, so being without my siblings in this house of horror was the worst form of punishment. My sister later told me that she would lie awake at night because she could hear me crying. She was so worried that something might be happening to me. I don't remember if anything was; I don't know. I guess God is good that way.

Before the social worker had taken us away, my mother told her, "My four children must stay together. All they have is each other." This was true. Together, we were tough and could get through anything, but apart, we were broken and weak.

My mother and father would call and check on us, but the calls had to be scheduled. We were very protective of our parents and knew, even back then, that we didn't want to worry them. We were always looking out less for ourselves than the people around us. We tried to act fine, and with the foster parents hovering over us during the calls, we would never want to say anything to upset them either.

However, our mother knew us so well. We were her babies. She knew in her heart something was wrong. She called the social worker and demanded, "They've got to get out. Something is off. Something is wrong over there!" The social worker paid us an unexpected visit and noticed we were in distress. We were not the same children they had left there ten weeks earlier.

Within a week of the surprise visit, two small-town police officers removed us and took us to another foster home further in the country and away from anything that was familiar.

Years later, when visiting my grandparents, I would look over at that house and at the woodpile my brother worked on. The house appeared unchanged. The curtains in the attic window remained, so I assumed it was the same owners.

I never told my siblings this, but as an adult, I reached out to those people. I looked up their number and called. When the woman answered, I said, "I'm not sure if you remember me." I told her that we were placed in their home in the early '80s.

She said, "I remember." She sounded happy, like nothing was wrong.

I told her how horrible that time was. I recalled exactly what happened on the first night of being there.

She said, "I'm very sorry." She explained that her husband had an issue with alcoholism. She then asked if she could put him on the phone. I reluctantly agreed, bracing myself for the sound of that stern voice that had scared me to my core as a child.

A familiar but more fragile voice said, "Hello." I recounted how he terrorized me as a little girl living in his home. He said he couldn't really recall some of the events, but he couldn't deny them either. He said, "I'm sorry, I was going through a lot back then. Can you forgive me?" And without hesitation, that's what I did—I forgave him. I knew that my forgiveness couldn't change the past, but it had all the power to change the future. I was calling them as a hurt person who wanted to understand why, and I hung up feeling sorry for them. I guess everybody is fighting a battle that we don't know about. It wasn't my place to judge. I like to leave those decisions up to God.

I can now drive past my grandparents' place without trying to avoid looking at the house across the road. There aren't as many hard feelings. I hope and pray that their family is in a better place as well.

In the second foster home, my silence helped me fly under the radar. I was no longer a target for punishment. Sadly, my brothers weren't so lucky. The parents in this home had other children as well, all boys. One evening, we all sat around the living room in our pajamas to watch *The Wizard of Oz*. Unfortunately, the movie wasn't enjoyable for my older brother Michael. He was petrified of the wicked witch. The foster family belittled him and called him names like "little baby Mike." He was sent to bed early that night for being a "baby." I remember at dinner when Michael dropped his fork with peas on the floor, and they made him eat his dinner in the bathroom for days because they said, "That was where pigs would eat." My brother Michael was always moving. I guess some would say he was hyper, but deep down, he was extremely sensitive. I cannot imagine how he felt eating dinner in the bathroom like an animal, but I do remember how I felt at the dinner table, looking at his empty seat next to me. I could feel his sadness from down the hallway, and it took all I had to hold back my tears. I saved them for when I was in bed at night. It was safer that way.

They were very unkind, and it was clear that we were a burden. The worst part was when the children of the home would taunt us: "Your mom is going to die. Your mom doesn't love you."

My little brother Mitchell had a blankie since birth. He carried it everywhere. It was quite shabby, but it was comforting to him. The older boys in the home dug a hole in the backyard and were laughing and thinking it was funny when they called us out there. They went to take the blanket from him. He was trying to hold on and pulled back with all his might, but Mitchell, who wasn't even in school yet, was no match for the preteen boys. After holding him down, they got the blanket from him. They made us watch as they buried it in their backyard. Mitchell never got his blanket back, but with God's perfect plan in place, he wouldn't need it. Instead, we would soon be wrapped in the warmth of God's grace. His angels were hard at work as we pulled up to meet our third and final foster family. My skies were no longer gray.

Chapter 9

REJOICE

The half-hour drive to our new foster home was filled with worry and uncertainty. This would be our third foster family. I wondered, *What will they be like? Will they be kind to us?* We had experienced the most petrifying, horrific, and abusive treatment in the previous two homes. Would this one be worse? I squeezed my little brother's hand when the social worker said, "We're almost there."

Days earlier, a wonderful couple, Calvin and Joyce Martin, had read a story in their local paper about a child who needed a foster family. The Martins had never fostered before. They had three daughters of their own: Camy, Suzy, and Annette. One daughter was out of the house and newly married; the other two were teenagers. God had blessed them with plenty, and they were dedicated to giving back. That evening, they had a family meeting about fostering the child they read about in the paper. The very next morning, Joyce called the department of social services. The social worker explained to Joyce that the boy had already been placed; however, they had four siblings who really needed a loving home, and it could be for quite a while. Four children were more than they had discussed, so Joyce called another family meeting. It was a lot to take on, but they trusted that God had chosen them because Joyce's phone call was just one phone call too late to foster the other child. With much prayer, they prepared for their loving family to grow by four.

When we pulled up to the Martins' home, immediately I was covered in a warm fuzzy feeling from the top of my head to the tips of my toes, a feeling I had never felt before. My eyes were as big as ever as we exited the social worker's car. Standing before us was a huge three-story white house with a wraparound porch. It was more beautiful than my daydreams had ever allowed. I glanced over at my siblings. My sister was also staring at the beautiful home with eyes as big as mine. My two brothers appeared in shock as their eyes were fixated on the massive boat in the driveway.

The side door to the beautiful house opened, and we were greeted with warm smiles. Calvin had white hair and a jolly demeanor. Joyce had the kindest brown eyes and a bright light illuminating from within her. I was in awe of her presence. She immediately bent down and swooped me up, probably assuming I was the youngest. I felt so safe in her arms. My siblings followed Joyce and me up the long staircase. "This is your home, and these are your bedrooms," she explained. We were taken aback; we had our own bedrooms! Still being held in Joyce's loving arms, she carried me into what would be my room. The bedding had flowers and was frilly and princess-like. Laid out on the bed were all these beautiful dresses. When I looked down, I gasped. There they were, lined up in a perfect row, little girl shoes and black-and-white saddle shoes. They were just like the ones I had dreamed about, the girl shoes I always prayed Jesus would slip on my feet—they were all right there. "And in the closet," she said, "these will be your special Sunday dresses." I felt like I was in a fairy tale. This was far beyond my daydreams and any vision I ever had for myself.

Calvin immediately took over, playing ball outside with my brothers. My sister was off with the Martins' youngest daughter, Annette. Michelle and Annette were instant buddies. There were other kids in this beautiful neighborhood, and they all came to welcome us. They would pull us around in their little red wagons, and when we'd play house, no one laughed at me for wanting to be Jackie Kennedy. Our new friends were wonderful, but I was happy just following Joyce around the big house.

I remember that first evening, before dinner, Joyce had us line up to wash our hands in the downstairs bathroom. I stepped up to the running faucet, and there it was on the sink, a pink round rose-shaped soap. It was the pink soap that I had always imagined. That's when my faith was reconfirmed to me. Jesus heard my lifetime of prayers, I believed.

Every morning, we woke up to a beautifully prepared breakfast. On worship mornings, we'd put on our Sunday best, which for me was now frilly dresses, white tights, and shiny shoes. For the first time, I felt like I fit in with the other girls in my Sunday school class, but only on the outside. Deep down, I never thought I was quite worthy of those nice things. I could get dressed up now on the outside, but my self-belief was tarnished, a burden I'd carry forever.

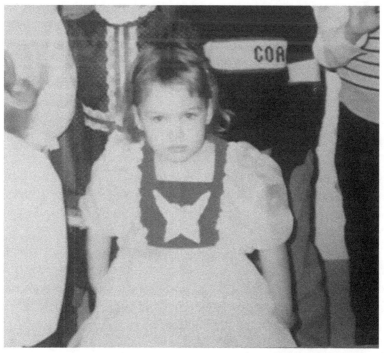

One Sunday, after church, as Joyce was helping me change into my play clothes, I gave her a big hug around her neck, and I asked her, "May I please call you mom?" She squeezed me back and replied, "Of course you can." My mother was okay with it too. I needed a parent to hold me in their arms and tell me everything was going to be okay, and Joyce did that for me.

I learned later that Joyce couldn't have children. Her three daughters were Calvin's from a previous marriage. She had taken care of the three girls since they were small, so she knew how to be a mother to children that weren't biologically hers. This gave her the ability to love me like a daughter. Maybe God never gave her children of her own so she could love others as if they were. I believe it was her spiritual calling. Our bond was very special, but I'm sure every child she ever cared for felt the same way.

Living with the Martins was nothing short of amazing grace. We were free to be kids without worry. My little brother loved to play in the mud, and Calvin and Joyce allowed him to do so. They had an extra shower in their basement, so he was free to play and get dirty. They would bring him in from outside and take him directly down to the shower. Regularly, we could hear Mitchell's squeals and giggles echo throughout the big house as he ran around the basement, making Calvin chase him.

The Martins took us on many exciting adventures. We enjoyed week-long vacations. On nice days, after church, we'd take their huge boat out on the lake. Cal, as I called him, allowed me to sit behind the wheel. He would whisper in my ear, "Turn the boat around and pretend we are going back to shore." Joyce and all the kids would start yelling, "What are you doing? It's not time to go back yet!" Cal would let out a belly laugh. "Good job, kiddo," he'd whisper to me with a high five. Cal helped me come out of my shell. I was free to be my silly self, pulling pranks on the family. There was nothing I loved more than a good old "I gotcha!"

At the dinner table, I always sat next to Cal, which got us into trouble more times than I can count. One evening, Joyce had prepared a spaghetti meal for us and some very important guests. The priest and nuns from the Catholic church where the Martins worshiped would also be joining us for dinner. My siblings and I sat up straight with our napkins gently placed in our laps. After saying grace, we attempted to eat with our best manners. It was not easy for children eating spaghetti, but we tried our best. Midway through our meal, Cal looked over at me and winked. I think he noticed how nervous and tense I was. Moments later, just as the priest was deep in conversation with them, Cal gently picked up my hand and dropped it in my plate of spaghetti. He then took my sauce-covered hand and placed it on my face. The entire table erupted into laughter, including the priest and nuns. Everyone except for Joyce, who scolded her husband, knowing she'd be the one cleaning up the mess. For the first time, I was the child being taken directly to the basement shower. From that evening on, every spaghetti dinner at the Martins ended the same way, but this time, I knew it was coming.

Christmastime with the Martins was as magical as any Christmas movie. The fireplace had stockings hung with all their names embroidered on them. It was obvious, the stockings had been in their family for years. That year, next to their old stockings, hung four new ones, beautifully embroidered with our names. Joyce stayed up for two nights straight, hand-making matching Christmas dresses for my sister and me. Michelle, always the tomboy and four years older than me, wasn't as thrilled as I was about our matching Christmas dresses. Nevertheless, I know she was grateful for Joyce's loving gesture.

On Christmas morning, Mitchell and I were the first to wake. We made our way down the hall, entering Michelle's and Michael's rooms with excitement. As a family, with overwhelming anticipation, we walked down the long staircase. Joyce and Cal had clearly been up long before us. The fireplace was lit, the stockings were stuffed, and there were wrapped presents from one end of the living room to the other. The presents and stockings were all so breathtaking, but the greatest gift the Martins gave us couldn't be bought and couldn't be wrapped. The true gift was what they restored within us—our faith in Jesus, our innocence, and our laughter. It truly was a time to rejoice.

Chapter 10

A Heavenly Promise

My siblings and I lived with Cal and Joyce Martin for one year. It was a year filled with countless blessings and lessons. During that time, my mother fought tirelessly to beat her illness and get back on her feet. She and my father had divorced. He was still working at a salvage yard. My mother was doing the best she could, but knew neither she nor my father was ready to fully provide for us.

Standing before a judge with the Martins and my father in the courtroom, my mother made a plea: "Please leave my four children in the care of the Martins until we can better provide for them. Please allow them to stay with this loving family a little longer." What my mother didn't know was that Joyce was tired. In a letter written to the judge just days before, Joyce had explained their predicament. She and Cal were older than my parents, and four small children were a lot of work. They loved us dearly, but after a year, they were simply worn out.

The judge heard my mother's plea and then asked her to please be seated. My father hadn't said a word. I think deep down he agreed with my mother—neither of them was ready.

Then the judge made a shocking ruling: "The children will be removed from the Martins effective immediately and placed in the care of their father."

The judge's decision had left my parents totally flabbergasted. My mother, especially, couldn't believe her ears. If she had known about the letter the Martins had written, she would have pled her case differently. She would have explained to the judge how she was better equipped than my father to care for us at that time. In speaking up, she unwittingly eliminated herself from getting us back, leaving the judge with no choice but to rule in favor of my father. As they were exiting the courtroom, my mother's shock had dissipated, replaced by anger and disbelief. She became enraged at the thought of us returning to a state of poverty and uncertainty—but this time without her care and protection. She couldn't bear the thought. As she was exiting the courtroom with her back to the judge, her emotions boiled over. She quickly spun around, throwing her purse across the courtroom aimed directly at the judge's head, screaming, "You don't know what you are doing!" as she was escorted out of the courtroom.

Joyce and Cal's daughters, Susy and Annette, were playing with us in the front yard when they returned from the courthouse. Unbeknownst to us where they were coming from, we ran into their arms and were greeted with smiles as always. But ever the observant child, it didn't make it past me that behind her smile, Joyce had been crying. Joyce took me in her arms and hugged me tight. I knew this feeling; it was familiar. This was goodbye.

She walked us to our rooms and began packing our clothing and toys. I sat on the bed with my feet dangling, studying her every move as she packed my pretty dresses and little girl shoes. She knelt down beside me and whispered, "Your dad will be here in one hour to pick you kids up." I immediately started to cry and asked, "Momma Joyce, why can't I stay here with you?" She replied, "I will always be with you, Melissa, forever." I would later learn that those weren't just words used to comfort me at the time; it was a promise, a promise like God's, a promise I could rest in, a promise she wouldn't break!

I remembered once seeing the old clothes we were wearing when we arrived at the Martins a year earlier; they were stashed away in a box in their basement. I don't know what my thought process was, but for some reason, I ran down to the basement and put them back on. I left my pretty clothes lying there on the concrete floor. Maybe somewhere deep down, I knew that the daydream was over. I was and always had been the little girl in hand-me-downs.

When my father arrived, we were happy to see him. He hugged us like a warm teddy bear. Sadly, his love and warmth wouldn't be enough.

We bid our tearful goodbyes to the Martin family. Joyce gave my sister a Bible with a beautifully written message on the inside cover, which I was unable to read until I was older because it was in cursive handwriting. They kissed our cheeks, and Joyce reminded us of Psalm 105:4: "Keep your eyes open for God, watch for his works; be alert for signs of his presence." Cal tussled my brother's hair and gave them pats on the back. He was saying goodbye to his boys. Their teenage daughters had tears rolling down their cheeks like we all did as we climbed into my father's beat-up car.

I remember watching through the rear window as the large beautiful white house shrank into the distance and quickly out of my sight. The situation was familiar to me, but I was changed. I had spent the last year living out my every daydream. I was the little girl in pretty dresses who smelled like flowers. My shoes were so shiny I could see my own reflection in them. For a moment in time, I lived like the little girls I had always admired. I now knew the true difference between the two worlds. Before being placed with the Martins, that kind of life was just a fairy tale. I now knew what I was missing, and that was more heartbreaking than never having it at all.

When we arrived at my father's apartment, he warmed up cinnamon rolls for dinner. There were just enough for each of us to have one, with only one remaining. Mitchell nearly choked scarfing down his roll so he could beat us to the last one. My father thought it was cute. He grinned and told Mitchell to hold his horses, but it wasn't cute to me. I was sad because I was aware that he had reverted to survival mode. I was looking at the same little boy who, out of hunger, buried his face into a bowl of applesauce over a year earlier, but my father wouldn't have known about that. When it was bedtime, there was no toothpaste for our toothbrushes that Joyce had packed, and there were no sheets on the mattresses. We were happy to be back in our father's loving arms, but it was obvious he wasn't ready to properly provide for us. We were back where we started but this time without our mother. She was right; the judge didn't know what he was doing.

While living with my father for almost a year, my mother was on a mission to get her life together in order to properly provide for us. She knew that the change in our lives had to start with her. She couldn't rewrite the past, but she held the pen and paper to write our futures. She was bound and determined to give us a better quality of life. After a tireless fight battling lymphoblastic leukemia, walking miles to and from her job, and attending night school at the local college, along with God's grace and the determination that only a mother could muster, we were finally returned to her care.

We moved into a small apartment without a stitch of furniture, but it would only be temporary. While working, my mother was also going to school to obtain her real estate license. I remember waking up to find her studying at all hours of the night.

My mother had pulled herself up by the bootstraps without receiving a helping hand. I was in awe of her grit, and I recognized that I, too, had some of that deep down within me. God didn't only create me in her image but also gave me her strength, and boy was I going to need it.

Chapter 11

THE IMPOSSIBLE DREAM

I n third grade, I was overjoyed to receive an invite to a classmate's birthday party and sleepover. It wasn't just any old invite. It was from the most popular girl in school. I no longer had to escape into their world; I was accepted into it.

With an overnight bag in hand, my mother dropped me off at the end of my classmate's driveway. I had envisioned that she lived in a big, beautiful home because of the way she was at school, and I was right.

I was greeted at the front door by the popular group of girls. They seemed as thrilled for me to be there as I was, but self-doubt quickly crept in as I wondered, *Is my gift going to be cool enough, and will she like it? Are my pajamas in style or dorky?* I gave the girls a good one-liner, and their laughter quickly silenced my insecurities. When in doubt, I went straight for the jokes. My sense of humor was where my confidence lived. Being funny was always my go-to, and I was good at it.

After enjoying cake and ice cream, the birthday girl decided we'd play a game of hide-and-go-seek in the dark. With the lights turned off, we all ran in opposite directions of the tri-level home. Everyone was searching for the darkest place to hide, and naturally, I followed the light. It led me to the den where a TV was on with no one watching. As a child, I didn't have many opportunities to watch television. Our black-and-white turn-dial was nothing like the big color set I found myself staring at. But it wasn't just the modern TV that caught my attention; it was what I saw on the screen that took my breath away. While the other girls were running around in the dark, I sat on the floor for nearly two hours, mesmerized. I was glued to the television. I had never seen anything like it, such eloquent beauty queens in their sparkling gowns. My mother was always beautiful in my eyes and in other peoples' eyes. I remember my mother never had fancy clothes when we were younger, but when we would walk into a public place, both men and women would pause when they glanced her way. She could stop a clock in any setting, but I had never seen my mother like that. The beauty contestants were stunning in their big rhinestone earrings, sequin gowns, and the highest of heels. A bomb could have gone off, and I still wouldn't have moved from watching the Miss USA pageant. I kept wondering, *How do these beautiful women do this? How did they get there to compete for the crown?* I wanted to know everything about it, so much so that after the sleepover, I went home and crumpled up my finished homework, a story I had to share with my class the next day. I rewrote that story. Instead, I wrote about what I had seen on television, about the dream that was laid on my heart in my classmate's den. I wanted to one day compete on the Miss USA stage. I wanted to wear a sequin gown. I wanted to wear the sash. I wanted it to say "Wisconsin" across my chest. I wanted to be beautiful like that.

The next morning, when it was my turn to get up in front of the class, I started to read about my dream when a boy whom I had a big crush on muttered under his breath, "Yeah, right." "She wants to be Miss Wisconsin," another kid said in a loud mocking tone. The other students joined in, laughing and pointing at me. I suppose it would seem impossible for someone like myself to one day become a beauty queen. I could feel the blood drain from my face as the teacher scolded the class and asked me to continue reading. It was at that moment I promised myself to chase the "impossible" dream with a vengeance.

Chapter 12

CAMPING IN CASHMERE

I n the spring of fifth grade, some of the students had an opportunity to go on a field trip to wilderness camp instead of attending school for the week, which was right up my alley. I mean, I had lived in a tent in the woods, so I could certainly master wilderness camp! It would be my first time away from my siblings for that many days, but I was excited. In fourth and fifth grade, I was becoming more popular, thanks to my sense of humor and silly personality. In March of fifth grade, I had won an award that I still have for being voted the nice girl in my class.

The wilderness trip was known as one of the biggest events of the school year. The teacher sent us home with a long list of camping items that we would need throughout the week: hiking boots, play clothes, a hat and gloves, a raincoat, and so on. The list was also specific about what we should not bring: no nice clothing, no jewelry, no scented soap or lotion, and no perfume or cologne. The paperwork explained that we would be hiking through the woods, tapping trees for sap, and looking for wildlife. If the animals smell your presence, they are less likely to appear—it makes sense.

I was overjoyed when my mother took me shopping for the specific items on the list. My mom was working part-time at night, bagging groceries. She was also working hard around the clock to build her career in real estate. She just sold a home and had made a commission check of one thousand dollars. It may not seem like a lot, but at that time, it was a big deal to us. For the first time in her life, my mother decided to invest in herself. So she went to a clothing store downtown, a place she wouldn't have dared to enter before. In the high-end boutique, she tried on items that she probably couldn't afford, knowing it would be essential in helping her real estate career. She purchased a cream cashmere sweater. It was fuzzy with huge shoulder pads. I know what you're thinking—huge shoulder pads!—but it was 1991, and they were an absolute must-have. She also picked out a silk shirt with pearl buttons (probably a hundred of them, from her neck, under her chin, all the way down to her waistline) and a pair of silk-lined dress pants pleated in the front. I know, but again, it was 1991. So here she was, looking like a million bucks in her new clothes, her suit coat with her Century 21 realtor pin. And to top it off, she sprayed herself down with a new perfume, lots of it. It was called Charisma, and it smelled nice but strong in a church lady kind of way.

The day had come. I was packing up all the essentials for wilderness camp. I was very excited but a little nervous. Once everything was packed, I put my bag in the back of my mother's station wagon that my siblings and I called "the grocery getter." My mother drove me to the parking lot where all the students who were taking the five-day trip were boarding the bus. I was one of the last students to arrive, so in a hurry, I said goodbye to my mother, grabbed my bag from the back of the "grocery getter," and handed it to the bus driver. He asked, "Is that it?" as he tossed it into the luggage compartment under the bus. I cheerfully answered, "Yes, sir!" I took the first window seat and waved farewell to my mother.

When we arrived at the wilderness camp, it was beautiful. We were deep in the woods. There was a large fire pit, hiking trails, and log cabins with bunk beds for us to sleep. After the bus driver unloaded our bags containing the specific items required, we met our college-age camp counselors. They showed us around and then back to our bunks. With the sun setting and a big week ahead of us, it was time to wash up and get ready for bed. Some students were already in their pajamas and waiting in line outside the restrooms with toothbrushes in hand when I sat down on the bottom bunk to unpack. I was so excited about the new gear and pajamas my mother had purchased. I carefully opened the bag and was immediately hit by an overwhelming scent. I recognized the intense fragrance. It was Charisma, my mother's new perfume, which, I must remind you, was prohibited. It took a moment for the pungent shock to wear off, and then reality set in. I started digging frantically through the bag. *Oh no,* I thought to myself, *how could this happen?* I realized that instead of my camping gear, I had brought my mother's dry cleaning, the fancy clothing she was going to be taking to the dry cleaner. She had them in the back of the car. I had grabbed the wrong bag!

Everyone was getting ready for bed, and I was thinking, *What in the world am I going to do? How am I going to pull this off?* I selected a few items that I thought I could sleep in, and I put them on. Everyone was staring at me like, "What is this girl doing?" but nobody said a word. So I washed up with a bar of soap in the bathroom and used my finger to brush my teeth.

That night, I didn't sleep a wink. I was busy planning how I was going to organize these fancy outfits to last me for five days. Not to mention, I was only fifty-nine pounds in the fifth grade, and these were women's clothing. My mother was petite at only five feet four and 110 pounds, but everything was way too big for me.

Early the next morning, the camp counselors rang the bell for us to get up and get dressed. There was a big hike planned, and I had decided the night before to wear the most shocking outfit first so after that it wouldn't seem so bad. Knowing how much my mother had paid for the clothes and how important they were for her career, I carefully put on the first outfit. There I was, overdressed, in cashmere with shoulder pads that were not on my shoulders but looked more like elbow pads. And to top it off, the itchy, fuzzy sweater had a shiny gold brooch pinned to it that I'm pretty sure was supposed to be at my chest and not my belly button. The bottom portion of my ensemble was a pair of pleated, silk-lined dress pants rolled at the top so they wouldn't fall down. I looked like I was auditioning for a part on the popular '80s show *Designing Women.* I was fully committed to pulling this off.

Then there was an announcement that everyone should go to eat breakfast in the cabin dining hall that was located at the center of the campground. I sashayed my way down the dirt trail and into the dining hall. Everyone was in line, getting their breakfast. There were students from many schools, not just mine, fifth graders from surrounding schools that I didn't know. They all stopped and stared at me. I could hear the young camp counselors whispering to each other. I was sure they noticed but probably didn't know how to handle the situation. I was thankful. It's like when a child closes their eyes and thinks you can't see them. I thought that if I just ignored everyone, nobody could see the obvious. I was sitting at breakfast, making it work, but the sweater was causing me to itch uncontrollably. After breakfast, we made our journey through the woods. I was watching the mile markers, one mile, two miles, and so on. I was burning up in the itchy cashmere sweater, and the silk-lined pants were making a noticeable swooshing sound with every step. Between the sound of the dress pants and the strong smell of perfume, our odds of seeing any wildlife were slim to none.

By day 3 of the wilderness camp, I was wearing my mother's Century 21 suit coat. The button was at my knees instead of my waist, so I had to shuffle like a mummy. My mother's Century 21 pin with her face on it was stitched to the lapel, and I couldn't remove it for the life of me. I looked like a fifth grader trying to sell real estate out in the sticks, and still, nobody was saying anything. That day, I shuffled through our adventures. That evening, we were all sitting around the campfire, roasting marshmallows, when suddenly there was an announcement over the intercom. "Attention, attention, Melissa Young [as soon as they said my name, I wanted to jump into the fire—this was it, I knew I was going down], your mother called and said that you accidentally took her dry cleaning instead of your clothes." That was it, there was no follow-up announcement. Everyone turned and started laughing and pointing and saying, "That's why you're dressed like that? They're your mom's clothes?"

There was no follow-up to the announcement, like: "She's on her way" or "She's coming to bring your clothes" or anything like that. It wasn't just an embarrassing moment; it was an embarrassing week-long event, and I still had Thursday and Friday to go.

The jig was up. I was wondering, *Now what am I going to do? Did they make the announcement just to let everybody know?* My mother, for some reason, called the camp just to inform me, like I hadn't noticed! It was day 3 for goodness' sake!

So I had to greet the next two days with everybody waiting in the breakfast hall to see what I was going to come walking down the dirt trail in. I was putting on a fashion show in my mother's dry cleaning with brooches and pearls that didn't fit and smelled of perfume.

To this day, I am not a fan of cashmere. It's a funny story that my family and friends get a kick out of. To quote my dear friend Kelly Hall, "Who doesn't wear cashmere to wilderness camp?"

At that time, I wholeheartedly believed that I was pulling it off until I was outed by the announcement. But upon reflection, I see the bigger picture. It goes back to kindergarten when I was walking to school across the frozen lake, wearing the shoes that I shared with my little brother. After the right one fell through the ice, the school nurse had found a left boot in the lost-and-found and told me, "You'll have to make do." Making do was all that I knew even though this time I wasn't in hand-me-downs—I was dressed to the nines, wearing the finest cashmere. I was still Melissa, not looking for anyone to fix it, not looking for someone to save the day. I was pushing through no matter the circumstances; I was still making do.

Chapter 13

RACING TO SUCCEED

When I was fourteen, my sister who is four years older than me had just graduated from high school and was planning to study police science and become a police officer. Michelle was always my protector. I looked up to her in many ways. She appeared strong on the outside while I hid my strength on the inside. Michelle and her longtime boyfriend became pregnant the summer after graduation. They are still married today with grown children and grandchildren. It turned out to be a wonderful story, but at that time, it was a huge bump in the road for her and a huge wake-up call for me. I was scared to death that any decision I made could take away the dream that I was clinging to for dear life, the dream that meant everything to me. Watching my sister become a young mother with a precious little boy and putting her future on hold helped me stay focused, not allowing anything to jeopardize my dreams. I thank her in so many ways because her bravery to keep her child, marry her high school sweetheart, and sacrifice her dreams helped to reinforce my dedication and pursuit of the "impossible" dream.

That same year, I begged my mother to take me to a local modeling agency. She finally gave in and made an appointment for me to meet with an agent after school. I was beyond excited. When we pulled up to the building, I could see a stylish woman peering through the large windows. From the moment we entered the office, the owner of the modeling agency couldn't take her eyes off my mother. She wanted to sign a contract with her immediately. She went on and on about how beautiful my mother was and how she resembled Jane Seymour. She asked what had taken her so long to break into the world of modeling. I sat in the chair, feeling completely invisible. I was always known for being "Micky's shadow." That's where I was the most comfortable, but in that moment, I wanted to step into the light. It was my dream that had brought us there, but it was my mother they wanted, and I didn't blame them. My mother was beautiful, the most beautiful woman I had ever seen. I probably should have known better and asked someone else to take me to the appointment. The agent signed my mother that day and suggested that I take modeling and acting classes to help me come out of my shell. My mother booked her first modeling job two days later, and I started taking classes. Although I wanted to begin working as a model immediately, the agent was right—I wasn't ready.

My Mom

My Mom

By the time I turned fifteen, I was signed with two modeling agencies. One was local, and the other was three hours away, in Chicago. I was finally a working model, making $45 to $95 an hour doing catalog shoots for major department stores. When you're fifteen, you think that's amazing even if you're only shooting for a couple of hours a week. My agent received 15 percent, and I saved the rest. The kids at school started to notice me in the newspapers on Sunday when they were flipping through, looking for whatever clothes they wanted. They would bring the ads to school and say, "Look, Melissa's in the paper." However, I wasn't saying much about my modeling. I was in the paper, and the kids started to think it was cool. However, I was no longer seeking their acceptance; I was on a mission to achieve much greater things in the shortest amount of time.

My mother drove me to every photo shoot. I valued those journeys just as much as I did modeling. I was able to share my dreams with her on those road trips. I talked about my visions of one day going to Hollywood, becoming an actress and a model. I believed this would be my ticket to compete for Miss Wisconsin, which ultimately could fulfill my greatest dream of standing on the Miss USA stage. My mother always said, "Melissa, you have such a sense of urgency, like there isn't enough time." She would tell me, "You're only fifteen. You have your whole life ahead of you to do this." But as always, I was following that inner voice, which I believe is the voice of God. I felt that there wasn't enough time for all the things I wanted to achieve. I needed to do them now. Unlike most teenagers who think they're invincible and have all the time in the world, I always felt like mine was running out.

Me Modeling at age 15

Chapter 14

ETERNAL LOVE

My maternal grandparents, Cliff and Nancy Kay, were an integral part of my adolescent years. Their deep devotion to God and unwavering love for each other was something I greatly admired. After all, my grandfather, in his teens, gave away his bicycle for a chance to get near my grandmother; and then they proceeded to have ten children together. Their love story played out like a classic romance movie, and all I knew was that I wanted to be loved just like that! Minus the ten children, of course.

After raising their large family, my grandparents enjoyed spending time with their many grandchildren. They also looked forward to traveling together. However, those plans were quickly interrupted by illness. In her late forties, my grandmother was sent to the Mayo Clinic in Rochester, Minnesota, after her small-town doctor couldn't put his finger on a diagnosis for her unusual symptoms. On her fifth day at Mayo, a specialist discovered a very rare glomus tumor measuring nine inches long, spanning from her jugular, through her middle ear, and to her brain. Surgery was imminent.

The invasive procedure took thirteen hours with five different teams of specialists. My grandfather never left her side. The thought of losing his beloved Nancy was too much for him to bear. Their children, including my mother, made the four-hour journey to Rochester in an RV and settled in at a campsite near the hospital.

My mother later shared with me how she could hear my grandmother's piercing screams echoing from down the long hallway. The pain was so horrific, she was begging to die. They had removed her eardrum along with the nine-inch tumor. She was cut from her throat to her brain. That area was completely hollowed out. They reattached her right ear for cosmetic reasons only. She was left with a huge scar, damage to a portion of her vocal cord, loss of hearing on her right side, and difficulty swallowing; but by the grace of God, she survived.

After a long and grueling recovery, my grandmother had a new lease on life. She didn't take one second for granted, not that she ever did. She still dressed up every morning, decked out from head to toe, wearing her big hats and jewelry. I remember her constantly asking if the clip-on earring was still attached to her right ear because she had no feeling there. She was a social butterfly, meeting up with friends and family at the local diner; and whenever possible, my grandfather took her out and led her around the dance floor while everyone gathered around to observe. My grandfather always looked at my grandmother the same way, like it was the first time he saw her, but now he held her closer and a little tighter. After she almost slipped through his hands and into the arms of God, he wasn't letting go.

My grandmother loved everything about my new adventures in modeling. She would often travel to Chicago with my mother and me. She was always there to cheer me on. I remember when I'd do runway shows on weekends, getting to bed late and having to wake up early on Sunday morning to find a Catholic church in the big city so she wouldn't miss Mass. I always knew if grandma was coming along, I wouldn't get any sleep, and I wouldn't have had it any other way. She also loved to play cards. She taught all her grandchildren how to play blackjack. There was always a lesson behind everything she did, and I can honestly say that learning when to pass, take a hit, or double down wasn't just about a game of cards—it was also about the game of life. Do you play it safe and pass, or do you keep going and risk it all? Either way, one face always shows, and the other one is hidden. It's not until the end that we see the whole picture.

My grandmother frequently returned to the Mayo Clinic for checkups. On one of those visits, the doctor discovered a small nodule on her lung that wasn't there before. They took a biopsy and called the family in to go over the pathology report. You could have heard a pin drop when the doctor said, "It's cancer." In my mind, I had a young and vibrant grandmother with a lot of life left to live. Her children and grandchildren were devastated, but for my grandfather, the terrible news was earth-shattering.

After her awful brain surgery and recovery, my grandmother couldn't fathom going through anything like that again. She made the difficult decision to not move forward with the treatment options that were offered. It was a decision not everyone agreed with, but it was honored and respected.

My grandfather became a man on a mission. He withdrew every dime they had, including the cash value of her life insurance policy. He took his beloved Nancy everywhere she wanted to go, including Las Vegas to try her luck at the blackjack table. When traveling became too difficult, he hired nurses to care for her in the comfort of their home.

Without treatment, the doctors gave my grandmother one year to live. A year and a half later, she was still fighting, getting dressed up, and making time for her many grandchildren. She was living each day to the fullest, promising, in her words, to go out with a bang.

The stress on my grandfather was visible. The effects of which culminated in a heart attack. While in a board meeting at work, he asked if they were ready to wrap things up. "I think I suffered a heart attack about thirty minutes ago," he explained to his coworkers. It was just like my grandfather to take care of business before taking care of himself. He underwent triple bypass surgery and returned home to my grandmother, whose health was failing.

Three weeks into his recovery, he heard my grandmother get up from her recliner and frantically rush out the front door. It was her physical response to not being able to breathe. Without thinking twice, he jumped to his feet and ran after her, lifting her collapsed body from their front porch step. She was rushed to the small-town hospital just a few blocks away. While the medical staff tended to my grandmother, my grandfather, in a blood-soaked shirt, stood at her side. The hospital staff didn't pay much attention to the blood, assuming my grandmother had been throwing it up, but it wasn't her blood—it was his. Recovering from bypass surgery, he had torn parts of his zipper-like incision while picking her up and holding her on the porch. His chest was torn open in more ways than one; both were the result of a broken heart.

That evening, surrounded by her family, my grandmother took her last breath; and in that very moment, you could hear loud booms thundering over the hospital. It was the Fourth of July, and just like she said she would, she went out with a bang. She was fifty-seven years old.

During one of our last conversations, my grandmother told me that when she gets to heaven, she'll be looking down on me. She said she'd be sitting at a blackjack table with the angels and bragging about all my achievements and how she was proud to be my grandmother. I cherished our last conversation. I'm sure she thought her words made me feel good about myself, but that wasn't the case. Instead, I felt the pressure of not letting her down. I couldn't leave her at the blackjack table in heaven with nothing to brag about. I was only fifteen years old, and this was another eye-opening event that fueled my ambitions to be somebody.

My grandfather, Cliff, passed away twenty years later. He never loved another woman after Nancy Kay. He woke up every morning and paid her a visit at the cemetery down the road. His name was carved in stone next to hers. He made sure he would be laid to rest on her left side so that she could hear him tell her, "I love you."

My Grandparents Cliff and Nancy

Chapter 15

On a Wing and a Prayer

Working diligently since I was fifteen years old, fueled by the dream that was laid on my heart in my classmate's den, after high school graduation and a few visits to Los Angeles, I decided it was time to make my move. My mother was heartbroken at the thought of me living so far away. She was newly remarried to Christopher, a wonderful man and single father with two daughters around my age. He was a natural caretaker, and I knew she'd be okay with him by her side.

My mother Micky and her husband Christopher

I packed my possessions into a small car, and with God as my only passenger, I fearlessly headed off to Hollywood, California, in search of the success I had always dreamed of.

It was the late '90s, and the internet wasn't what it is now, so I secured an apartment over the phone, sight unseen. I was about to learn a valuable lesson on the importance of location, location, location! All I knew was that the other apartments I inquired about were way out of my price range. I had saved every dime, and this one was more within my budget. After a long three-day journey, I finally made it to Los Angeles. It was nightfall, and I was excited about meeting the apartment manager and obtaining the keys to my new place. I had stayed with a few roommates before, but I had never lived on my own over two thousand miles away from home. It was just me and my dreams.

As I drove through the seedy neighborhood, at every stoplight, people were approaching my car, trying to get me to roll down the window. I had been homeless before, but this was awful. I would have taken that tent in a Wisconsin park over this any day. I was fearless when I left Wisconsin, and now, I was petrified. While walking up to the apartment building, I noticed what would be my mailbox. It looked like someone had taken a drill to the keyhole. There were bars on the windows, and from the apartments overhead, men were yelling obscenities at me. The foul language didn't penetrate my thick skin, but their threatening tone scared me to my bones. My hands were trembling as I knocked on the door of apartment number 3. "Please hurry up and answer," I whispered to myself as two young men covered in facial tattoos were approaching my direction. I was a sitting duck standing outside, looking like I came from Mayberry.

When the manager finally opened the door (wearing a surgical mask), the strong smell of bleach hit me like a Mack truck. It was so intense my eyes were burning to tears. Someone had generously scrubbed the place from top to bottom. I'm certain, at some point, the apartment was the home of a crime scene. The manager proceeded to give me the grand tour using a battery-powered spotlight because there was no electricity. The ceilings in the closets were cut out large enough to fit a body or two. He explained that the holes were a result of the police searching for contraband. In the bedroom, there was a mattress lying on the floor—I will spare you its description. Anyway, the manager graciously offered, "You can keep the mattress if you give me fifty bucks for it." I started to cry. "I can't live here," I told him. "I'm pretty sure I'll come up missing. I'll be on the six-o'clock news tomorrow." He just grinned, but I was dead serious. I was so scared I didn't want him to leave before me. I quickly handed him the keys back and didn't wait around long enough to retrieve my security deposit. I was just praying to God that my car carrying my possessions was still parked out front and all in one piece.

I sped out of there and went straight to a hotel. The next morning, I called another place from a rental booklet I found in the hotel lobby. It was a teeny-tiny apartment. There was just enough room for a twin bed and a refrigerator next to it. There was no kitchen, just a stand-up shower and toilet. It was essentially a closet, measuring around fourteen-by-ten feet. But it was clean with a gated courtyard, and I couldn't have been more grateful. They wanted $750 a month for the little hole in the wall, and I happily took it. After all, I was a master at "making do." Next door, on one side of the apartment was a church, and on the other side was the police department. I knew I was in good hands. I had the Lord and the law on each side, so I was covered. Looking back, I think it might not have been legal to rent; it seemed more like a corner storage room with a bit of carpet and some paint. It didn't compare at all to the other apartments in the building, but it was mine, and I loved it.

Before I left Wisconsin, my modeling agency had signed me up to take acting classes in Hollywood. The first day, I was sitting in class with a notebook and pencil, writing down everything the teacher said. He started talking about an agency that represented a lot of young actors, many of which were on popular television shows. As soon as he mentioned it, I wrote it down and thought, *So what am I sitting in this class for? I should be going to that agency. I'm wasting precious time.* Again, that inner voice was ever so present, telling me there wasn't enough time.

The next morning, instead of returning to acting class, I decided to make my way to the talent agency that I had written down. When I entered the building, I was greeted by a beautiful but stone-faced receptionist. While looking past me, she asked, "Can I help you?"

With excitement in my voice and wearing a great big smile, I responded, "Yes, ma'am. May I please meet with an agent?"

She laughed out loud and explained, "You can't just come in here and see someone. You need to have an appointment. Did you send us an acting résumé and headshots? We call you and decide if we want to see you or not."

I thought to myself, *I came all this way, and I have nothing to lose.* It was 9:00 a.m., and I was already missing acting class. I explained to the receptionist, "I'll hang out here for a while just in case."

"Where are you from?" she asked.

I proudly responded, "I'm from Wisconsin, ma'am."

She giggled and muttered under her breath, "Well, that explains a lot."

I was a little embarrassed because I wasn't just unprepared, I was unqualified. In class, I had written down the agency's name, but I hadn't written down all the things I needed to do in order to be ready to walk into this situation. That was probably what I was missing in acting class that day.

As I grabbed the nearest chair, I whispered, "I'll just sit right here if you don't mind, and maybe someone will have a free moment to see me." The clock had now turned to 10:00 a.m. She picked up the phone, and I could hear her making fun of me to the person on the other end. People were now peering out of their offices to get a look at me sitting there with my modeling photos in a black zip-up case on my lap. I kept my head up, pretending I didn't know what she was doing. I was committed at this point. Like always, once my mind is made up, there's no talking myself out of it.

The hours went by, and out of the corner of my eye, through a window, I could see my car on the street—it was being ticketed. I didn't want to go out and move it because I was worried she would lock the doors behind me. I sat in the waiting room for the entire day. Like a fixture on the wall, I watched at least a dozen people with appointments come and go. The agents left their offices and returned with Starbucks—I assumed it was their lunch break. As they walked past me, they giggled. I had become the office entertainment, and I was perfectly fine with that. I could handle people laughing at me; it wasn't the first time. As long as they weren't looking at me with pity, I was good. I don't do pity.

When three o'clock rolled around, I started thinking, at this point, I might have to take the walk of shame. But again, there was that inner voice saying, *I've come this far, and it's going to happen for somebody, so why not me? Why not?* So I stayed glued to my chair. I had nothing to lose, and I couldn't leave without knowing I had tried my best.

It was the end of the day, and everyone was packing up and leaving when an agent walked up to me and introduced himself. He said, "You've been sitting here all day."

I stood up and shook his hand. "Yes, sir, I didn't have an appointment, but you see, I have this big dream of one day competing in the Miss USA pageant, but I need experience with modeling and acting. I've been preparing for this all my life, and I was told that you are the best to help me get there," I replied all in one breath.

He stopped me. "Whoa, slow down. Okay, you are either crazy or you want this really bad."

I replied, "Maybe I'm a little of both, but I want this really, really bad!"

My response made him laugh. He said, "I'll be right back."

In a joking manner, I replied, "I'm not going anywhere."

He responded with his back to me, "I'm aware of that."

He returned a moment later, carrying a piece of paper. In the waiting room with the receptionist and agents gathered around, he explained, "I want you to read this monologue for all of us right here." I knew he was trying to humiliate me out the door. I looked down at the piece of paper, and the scene was from *Forrest Gump* when Sally Field is telling Forrest that she is sick. I loved that movie and had seen it in the theater with my mother years earlier. He asked me to look it over, assuming I had no idea what the words were. Setting me up to fail, he said, "I'll give you sixty seconds to study it, and then I want you to act it out." I didn't need sixty seconds. I glanced at it for maybe twenty seconds, turned it upside down, and set it on the chair where I had been sitting all day. Little did he know, I knew that scene very well.

For a moment, in a waiting room full of strangers, I was Sally Field saying goodbye to her son. The room went completely silent. The agent turned around and walked away. Everyone was staring at me as I awkwardly gathered my things to leave. As I slowly took my walk of shame, heading for the door, I heard the gentleman's voice from behind me, "Okay, okay, you have an audition tomorrow at CBS for a soap opera. Don't be late!" I turned back and gave him a big hug. He said, "Here's the info, now go on and get out of here."

Modeling photos at age 19

The next morning, I arrived on time at the studio, excited and nervous. I told the parking attendant that I had an audition. He looked at me like, "Big deal." I'm sure he was used to seeing big-name actors and actresses every day. Who was I? Looking back, I would have rolled my eyes at me too. I entered the huge building and took the elevator to the correct floor. The walls were covered with photos of famous actors I recognized from TV shows and commercials. I turned the corner, and there was a long line of young women around my age waiting in the studio hallway, ready to audition. That's when it hit me—it wasn't just me that had an audition. It was everyone and their neighbor. I was so naive. I didn't know the process. I thought that I was the only one auditioning that day.

I was in awe of the other young women; they had such beauty and poise. They were what I had always imagined young women in Hollywood looked like. No one looked like me with my fair skin and short black hair cut above my ears. I felt the urge to turn around and run back to the elevator, but remembering how I waited in that room the day before, I knew I had to stay the course.

A woman started walking down the hall, robotically handing out pieces of paper that said what the role was for; our lines were also attached. I looked down at the paper and was shocked at what I read.

The character is a seventeen-year-old high school student from a small town in Wisconsin. Not believing my eyes, I read it again. Could this really be happening? "This is me!" I accidentally blurted out loud. "No, it's me," the girl in front of me proclaimed. She was already in character and thought it was some sort of competition, but I was saying, "It's me," for real!

I went into the audition in my Wisconsin friendly way, the only way I know how to be; I walked straight up to the casting director and staff sitting behind the long table and reached out to shake their hands. They quickly corrected me, "You're not supposed to approach the table. Just stand there on the X where the camera is focused on you and say your lines." I was a little thrown off. I didn't want to be rude and not shake their hands, but I did what they asked. I read my lines, and they said, "Do it again," so I did. They said, "Okay, thank you. You can leave now." I figured that was that. I had tried my best, but I realized I was completely out of my element and I had a lot to learn.

When I arrived back at my apartment, I had two blinking messages on my answering machine. The first one was from my mother asking how it went. The second one was from the agent I had met the day before. He said, "Congratulations, Melissa, you got the part."

I wasn't a big TV star or anything like that, but I got to be in a lot of scenes, some in the background. My family and friends back home could see me. Sometimes we'd shoot at Fairfax High School in Los Angeles. The studio would bring in truckloads of fake-colored fall leaves to make it look like autumn in Wisconsin. The show took place in a fictional town in Wisconsin, and I felt like I was back at home for a moment. It was the best of both worlds.

MELISSA YOUNG

My first acting comp card while living Los Angeles

Within my first full week of living in Los Angeles, another actress who was about my age and was also from the Midwest, offered to take me out for a drink. I wasn't old enough to get into a club, but she explained that it was a Cuban restaurant with live salsa music and dancing, so I agreed.

We walked into Havana on Sunset Boulevard. It was a Tuesday night, and there was a guy in a white shirt and black bow-tie holding a towel in his hand, drying the top of the bar. He glanced at us and dropped the towel onto the floor. He was staring at me. I was thinking, *Oh no, he knows I'm underage. I'm definitely not going to order an alcoholic drink.* I didn't want to get thrown out.

There was a salsa band playing, and the man with the towel came over and asked us if we wanted their signature mojito. I nervously took him up on his offer, praying to God he wouldn't ask for my identification. I thought he was very handsome, and

I couldn't help but watch him from across the room. Shortly, he made his way over with our drinks. He kept coming back to our area, finding excuses, lighting candles, and rearranging things, all the while looking my way. After slowly sipping my mojito, afraid of being found out, the handsome bartender asked if I would like another drink. I nervously answered, "No, thank you, sir."

He said, "Close, my name is Sergio."

Sergio asked very confidently, "Would you like to salsa dance with me?"

I'm known for having two left feet, so I immediately turned down his offer. "No, thank you. I don't know how," I replied.

He explained that he was taking lessons and would love to teach me. I finally gave in to his persistence and agreed to join him on the dance floor. I'm pretty sure the mojito played a part in my decision. The young woman who had invited me out for a drink decided to call it a night.

Sergio closed up the bar and taught me how to salsa dance. We enjoyed each other's company (only in conversation of course) until 1:00 a.m. I shared what life was like growing up in a small town in Wisconsin, and he shared the obvious contrast to his life growing up in the City of Angels. I explained what brought me to the big city. I told him about my dream of one day standing on the stage at Miss USA. He said, "I believe in your dream, and I look forward to watching you compete in the pageant on television." Sergio had a huge smile, not just because he was happy but because God had created it that way. I was completely smitten by the tall dark-haired man. I hadn't met anyone like him back home. He was worldly, well-traveled, and fluent in three languages. I was as green as a girl could be, and he was the complete opposite. He had seen it all. His parents were immigrants from a small town outside of Mexico City. They came to America to give their family a better life. He was proud to be in this great country, and I was honored to be in his presence.

As the night came to a close, Sergio asked me for my number. I remembered my mother's warning: "Don't give out your number or address to anyone. Take theirs instead." He was a perfect gentleman all evening, but as always, I followed her advice. "I can't give you my number, but I can take yours," I replied. I think he took it as a rejection, but that wasn't the case. By this time, my ride was waiting. As Sergio walked me to the car, one of his coworkers offered to snap a photo of us to document the memorable evening. Then he opened my door and said, "Goodbye." There was no kiss. Our only exchange was his number and a smile. As the car pulled away, I could see him out of the rear window. There he was all alone, standing in the middle of the parking lot with a sad look as if he were saying goodbye forever. All he was left with was a crooked photograph taken underneath the Havana sign, holding the young woman from Wisconsin.

Sergio and I underneath the Havana sign on the night we met

That Friday, around closing time, I walked back into that Cuban restaurant on Sunset Boulevard. I saw Sergio first; he looked down in the dumps. As I made my way across the room, his coworkers started cheering, "She's here, she came back!" Sergio stopped what he was doing and ran over to me. With a big hug, he said, "I'm never letting go of you again." From that moment on, we were inseparable.

Sergio opened my eyes to a whole new world, and at the same time, I was opening his eyes to the world he took for granted. For instance, I always wanted to see the Hollywood sign up close; he offered to take me. As we were sitting at the Griffith Observatory, he mentioned that it was the closest view he had ever had of the sign as well. Sergio became my tour guide, but unbeknownst to me, I was giving him a closer look at the city he called home—the city that for him had become nothing more than a backdrop. On clear days, he took me for long drives up the Pacific Coast Highway in his little black sports car, all the while listening to "Angels" by Robbie Williams repeatedly on the stereo. He introduced me to different cultures, taking me to his favorite Japanese restaurant in Pasadena, where I fell in love with sushi. He was fluent in Japanese, and we always received the best service after he spoke with the chefs in their language.

Some of my favorite times were spent with Sergio's family. They primarily spoke Spanish. However, it's been said that only seven percent of communication is verbal, and although I couldn't understand their words, I could feel their love. Sergio's grandmother Anastacia always prepared something for me to eat, whether I was hungry or not. I will never forget when she mistakenly added paprika instead of cinnamon to my French toast. Never one to be picky, I ate it with a smile but declined her generous offer for seconds. His mother, Lina, would pick up extra items at the market to fill my bare cupboards so I wouldn't go without. His father, Justino, had the warmest smile and the pride he exuded, for his son was palpable. His brother, Jose, was a projectionist at a theater on the Third Street Promenade in downtown Santa Monica. He would generously give us movie tickets to see the newest blockbuster hits. Jose's longtime girlfriend, Maria, and I always enjoyed a good laugh at the two brothers' expense. I was in love with Sergio's family just as much as I was with him.

The only time Sergio and I were apart was when we were working. The cost of living in Los Angeles was and still is insanely expensive. My acting and modeling jobs didn't cover all my bills, so I got a job working thirty hours every weekend, selling suits at a men's clothing store. It was a great fit because it left my weekdays open for auditions and the work that came from them. I didn't know anything about retail, especially men's suits. It was all men working there, except for me and Annie, the sweet woman who kind of ran the place and worked behind the register. There was a tailor named Jack, who did alterations in the backroom. I felt an instant connection with him. I spent most of my breaks chatting with him while he sat behind his sewing machine. From day 1, I told him how much I loved his name. I explained my adoration for Jack and Jackie Kennedy and how, as a child, they played a starring role in my daydreams.

My coworkers at the suit store became like family to me. Annie treated me like a daughter, always offering up her motherly advice and making sure I was doing okay. "Did you get enough sleep last night?" and "Did you have enough to eat for lunch today?" were just a few of the common questions she'd ask. Annie made me promise that I wouldn't allow the big city to change me, and I was committed to keeping my word. I adored Annie and always looked forward to seeing her smiling face and being embraced by her warm hugs. The men whom I worked alongside on the sales floor were like brothers, always watching out for me. When Sergio would come around for a quick visit or to pick out some new threads, they'd give him a hard time, just like my biological brothers would have done back home.

My weekend job was a blessing, not just financially but in many ways. In Los Angeles, a young woman could easily get into a lot of trouble on the weekends. But for me, instead, those weekends at the suit store were almost like going home. There is no doubt that God put those wonderful people in my life when I needed them the most, just another example of how He watches over me.

My coworkers at the men's suit broker, Annie and Jack the tailor

I went to every audition, acting and modeling job that presented itself (except the inappropriate ones, I graciously passed on those). I shot a lot of commercials, some national and some local. I was an extra on more television shows than I can count, and sometimes, I got lucky enough to have a speaking role. I was doing exactly what I had set out to do. I was a working model and actress, living on my own, and I had a boyfriend who I was madly in love with. However, there was one mission I had yet to accomplish, a dream that was tattooed on my heart since third grade, a dream that wouldn't go away.

After three years, Sergio came to me and said, "Melissa, I want to marry you someday, and I'm afraid you'll resent me if you don't go back to the state that you love and compete for Miss Wisconsin and just try to see if you can win. You told me when we first met that you wanted nothing more than to stand on the Miss USA pageant stage."

The pageant rules stated that you couldn't be married or have had any children, and at that time, the cutoff age was twenty-six. He said, "You're going to have to go back home and give it your best shot, and I'll go with you." I knew he was right. I was doing well in Los Angeles, and I loved it there. I was finding myself and coming into my own, but this was what I had been waiting for all my life. I was as ready as I was ever going to be.

Sergio's whole world was in Los Angeles, and he was willing to leave it all for me. I was a little scared to go back home and leave the place where I felt, for the first time, I was becoming successful. I had worked very hard for it. To leave it all for the small chance that I might be the one chosen, I was once again willing to lose everything to gain it all.

But now it wasn't just me that was giving something up. Sergio was leaving behind the only life he knew for my shot at achieving a childhood dream, the dream that I was always told would be impossible.

Chapter 16

THIS IS THE MOMENT

A fter three years living on my own, it was time to leave the big city where I was blessed with countless God-incidences and tremendous personal growth.

Sergio sold his classic 1966 Mustang and packed his belongings into his small sports car. He bid a tearful farewell to his family and drove over to my apartment. It was empty, just like the day I found it. My belongings were packed tightly into the same car that had brought me there years earlier. The only thing that had changed was me. I learned a lot about myself while living in that tiny, closet-like apartment. It was within those four walls that I got to know myself and what I was made of. With two CB radios, Sergio in his car and me in mine, we left the city of Angels and made our way north, back to where I came from. What would be a new world for him was just a familiar old place to me. The tables had turned, and I was now his tour guide.

My family was overjoyed to have me back. Sergio and I rented an apartment just outside my hometown to reestablish my residence. I could have competed in the Miss California USA pageant—it would have been a heck of a lot easier to stay put instead of packing up both of our lives—but that was not my dream. My dream was to compete in the state where I grew up, where I was told it would be impossible for me to achieve.

My dream was to stand on the Miss USA pageant stage with the Wisconsin sash proudly draped across my chest.

After returning home, I immediately started preparing for the Miss Wisconsin USA pageant. I grew out my hair and went to the gym every day. I never had a pageant coach; at the time, I couldn't even tell you what one looked like. As always it was just me and my dream.

The weekend before the pageant, all of us contestants were given a number to wear on our hip for the judges to identify us for proper scoring on stage and in personal interviews. I was so excited when I received mine. I was number 59. The numbers five and nine have always been meaningful to me. I was born in the fifth month, on the ninth day. The Bible verse Job 5:9, "He performs wonders that cannot be fathomed, miracles that cannot be counted," was one of my favorites. Was it a sign? Maybe, maybe not. I saw the lucky numbers as a blessing, but on the flip side, having number 59 also meant that there were so many women vying for the crown.

With blind faith and a competition gown worth less than one hundred dollars, it was finally pageant weekend, a moment I had been praying and waiting for all my life. I met all the wonderful contestants while we waited outside the conference room where the judges conducted our personal interviews. They were incredibly beautiful and poised.

We spent the next day rehearsing for the onstage preliminary competition, introductions, evening gown, and swimsuit. I was becoming fast friends with the other contestants; it never felt like a competition because I wasn't there competing with anyone else. I was in competition with myself and the doubt I had carried since childhood. I was trying to outdo my past, not the other women.

After the preliminary competition, I was flooded with emotion. The weight of every expectation I had for myself was resting on my shoulders. It all came down to this moment.

The final day of competition had arrived. As we all took the stage, I could see my family perfectly in the audience; all of them showed up. They were wearing buttons with my picture and cheering as loud as they could from the sixth and seventh rows.

It was time to announce the special awards.

"All the contestants voted, and the Miss Congeniality award goes to . . . number 59, Melissa Young!" the MC announced. It was a huge honor. I was moved to tears by my fellow pageant sisters' decision.

The scores were in, and they were ready to announce the top ten. As they called one woman after another, I noticed they all had something in common—they were all blondes. I thought to myself, *I'm not at all what they're looking for.* Just as the self-doubt was speaking to me, the MC announced, "With only two spots left, the next contestant is . . . number 59, Melissa Young!" I did it! I was in the top ten! I couldn't feel my feet touch the stage as I glided over to join the finalists. Next, the tenth woman was called to round off the top ten; she was blond as well. I was the only brunette.

Did they just throw me in here to make it seem a little more balanced? I wondered. Either way, I wasn't eliminated yet, and I tend to do my best when the odds are stacked against me.

It was time for the legendary final question. In pageants, it's often the final question that can make or break you. When it was my turn, Mary Clarke, the wonderful MC, took my hand before asking me my question. She could see how badly I was trembling. I squeezed hers back so tightly, I'm surprised I didn't do damage. With our hands locked together, she asked me about being awarded Miss Congeniality, how I felt, and what it meant to me. My nerves disappeared, and I eased my grip from Mary's hand. I explained, from my heart, how I was touched, how it was the best award I'd ever received, how I'll always look at it and think about my time with these beautiful women, and how I was honored to be in their presence and now to call them my dear friends.

All the contestants that didn't make it into the top ten were now in the back of the audience and watching the rest of the pageant. As I finished answering my question, they started screaming and cheering for me. Their enthusiasm became infectious throughout the ballroom.

The moment had come to narrow the finalists down to the top three. To my surprise, I made the cut! I felt weak in the knees as they called my name. The lights were so bright at that point, I couldn't see my mother's face. I was wondering what she was thinking and feeling. I didn't know it was possible, but at that moment, I wanted it more than ever before. There I was in the final three, standing among two remarkably beautiful and intelligent women; in my eyes, there was no chance that I could be the one chosen. I never attended a university; these women had. They were well on their way to becoming huge successes in life. All I had was this big dream and a whole lot of heart.

They announced the second runner up; it wasn't me. There were just two of us left, a stunning young woman named Summer and me. We held hands and faced each other. She leaned in and gently whispered, "Get ready, Melissa. It's going to be you." I shook my head.

No, it just can't be. I can't believe I'm standing here. I could hear my father shout my name from the audience; I could hear my whole family cheering, *"Melissa!"* I could barely hold my body up while holding Summer's hands, waiting for the verdict. The auditor was tallying the final scores while pageant director, Jim Clingman, was singing a beautiful rendition of "This Is the Moment."

I looked down and slightly over my right shoulder, like someone had tapped on it. I could see myself standing there as a little girl—in my hand-me-downs with torn boy shoes, who often went to bed hungry, the little girl who slept in an attic after being beaten by a foster parent. She was as clear as day. My heart was racing because I wanted this so badly for her.

As Mr. Clingman hit the final high note with "This is the moment, the greatest moment of them all," there wasn't a dry eye in the house. As he exited the stage, I shook off the vision of my younger self, then the MC announced, "And the first runner up is . . . number 47!" I glanced down at the button on Summer's hip and saw that it was her number. Then the words I had waited nearly all my life to hear echoed throughout the ballroom: "And the winner is . . . Melissa Young!"

Wait, had I heard them correctly? Was it really me? I was afraid to celebrate, believing there was some sort of mistake.

I turned to the MC and then to judges and asked, "Is it me? Is it me?" while pointing to my chest. She answered, "Yes, congratulations!"

The outgoing Miss Wisconsin walked toward me with the crown and sash. As she literally helped me walk to the center of the stage, the ballroom erupted. I still couldn't believe it. So many people had to confirm, "It's you!"

When it finally sank in, the celebration was so big and so great, I could barely contain myself. Moments before, when the scores were counted, a member of the pageant staff noticed I was going to win. She ran backstage and told the pageant directors, Jim and Judy Clingman, "You're going to want to come out from behind the curtain to see this because this woman has absolutely no idea that she is about to win." So everyone had come out from behind the stage to witness my reaction.

When I turned around after hugging the outgoing Miss Wisconsin, I saw the judges giving me a standing ovation. One of them had her eyeglasses in her hands because she was crying so hard. The former titleholder put the crown on my head and the sash over my right shoulder. The MC handed me roses and a trophy and said, "Take your walk, Miss Wisconsin."

As I started to walk down the runway, through my tears and the bright lights, I could see my mother and father hugging and sobbing in an embrace I had not seen since I was a little girl. I had just won the title, but it was a victory for everybody, my siblings, and my parents. When I got to the end of the stage, I saw Sergio standing on his seat, six rows back (he later explained it was because he wanted to stand so tall for me).

I took that trophy and shot it into the air like a prize fighter who had just gone the distance to win the title. It wasn't proper for a beauty queen, maybe even unladylike, but it was me, and it was exactly how I felt at that moment. I had just earned my ticket to compete on the Miss USA stage.

Photo credit Michael Solberg

On October 31, 2004, with blind faith, hard work, and heart, I turned an impossible childhood dream into reality as I was crowned Miss Wisconsin USA 2005. It was one of the best moments of my life. It was like my favorite *Rocky* poster, which reads, "His whole life was a million-to-one shot." That was true for me as well. I was Rocky at that moment, an underdog who beat the odds, fought the struggles of life, and finally won.

Later on, one of the judges said to me, "Melissa, your scores were so high in personal interviews that no matter what—it didn't matter that your gown was inexpensive and it was falling off, and you had to hold it up as you walked across the stage. None of that mattered because you had won for who you are on the inside. We can change a contestant's hair and wardrobe, but we can't manufacture their spirit."

I was so unsure and doubting something that was already mine. The truth is, it was mine when I was a little girl, and I didn't know it because no matter what, I was going to make it happen. I wish I had given myself a little bit more reassurance and not been so hard on myself.

One of my most treasured moments happened a few days later. Calvin and Joyce Martin, the beloved couple who welcomed my siblings and me into their family after two abusive foster homes, read about my victory in the newspaper. They called to congratulate me and invited me home for a celebration. Joyce was like a proud mama, bragging to everyone that her daughter was Miss Wisconsin. It was a far cry from the little ragamuffin who followed her around like a lost puppy. God's grace is truly remarkable.

Menasha woman wins Miss Wisconsin USA

THE NEWS-RECORD

MENASHA — Melissa Young was happy just to compete at the Miss Wisconsin USA pageant last weekend.

The 25-year-old Menasha woman wasn't expecting to be crowned Miss Wisconsin USA 2005.

But that's exactly what happened.

Young won the pageant at Wisconsin Dells Sunday night. By winning, she earned the right to compete in the Miss USA pageant in Baltimore, Md., in April.

Young, a 1998 graduate of Menasha High School, said she was "ecstatic" that she emerged as the winner of the Wisconsin pageant.

The weekend-long pageant included one-on-one interviews with judges, an evening gown competition, swimsuit event and on-stage interviews.

Young, who also was named Miss Congeniality, said she was thrilled just to make the top 10. Winning the competition was beyond her expectations, she added.

"It was the most exciting thing of my life," she said. "My friends and family were there. It was amazing."

Young was among 40 women from Wisconsin who competed at the state pageant. She is looking forward to the Miss USA competition next April.

"I'm so excited," she said.

Young

The mayor of my hometown presented me with the key to the city and alderman, James Taylor, put up a sign, eighteen feet long, that read "Home of Melissa Ann Young, 2005 Miss Wisconsin USA." In the town where I was once a little girl going nowhere, you couldn't drive off the highway without seeing that sign; it remained there for over ten years, right in front of our football stadium. All those kiddos in the third grade who pointed and laughed at my dream were now grown up and had to drive past that sign to work and their homes every day.

When the hometown football team asked me to come to their final game and sign autographs, I brought one hundred photos to sign, but the line of people far exceeded that. They had to take down names and addresses so I could send them by mail. I did a double take when a handsome man kindly asked for my autograph, I quickly recognized him as the boy who said, "Yeah right!" when I shared my dream with my classmates in the third grade. I was crushed back then, but now, there he was, standing in the cold, waiting for my autograph. His eyes were so kind as he smiled at me. He said that I should be proud of my accomplishments.

It was right then and there that I realized, chasing this dream had nothing to do with the kids who made fun of it but everything to do with me and how I felt about myself at that time. I wasn't trying to prove I was good enough to them; I was trying to prove it to myself. I used their laughter as my rocket fuel, and if nothing else, I owed them a debt of gratitude.

On April 11, 2005, on live television in front of 250,000,000 viewers in more than seventy-five countries, I made history. For the first time in fifty-four years, Miss Wisconsin was voted Miss Congeniality. Also, for the first time in pageant history, it was a unanimous decision!

Receiving the award on stage.

Me and boxing legend Sugar Ray Leonard

Sergio and I

I'll never forget the moment when Donald Trump, then the owner of the Miss Universe Organization, approached me onstage, shook my hand, and said, "Nice to meet you, Miss Personality"—a pivotal moment that would change history forever. It was at that time that I also received a check from the Trump Organization for $1,000 for winning the hearts of my fellow competitors. Little did I know, that check would soon take me back to my humble beginnings and teach me a life-changing lesson in forgiveness.

Wisconsin's **Melissa Young**
named national "Miss Congeniality" winner at
MISS USA PAGEANT

Miss Wisconsin-USA 2005, Melissa Young was selected by the 50 other state contestants in this year's **MISS USA PAGEANT** as the most liked among the group. Congratulations on this much-deserved honor, shown here receiving the award on the live NBC telecast. On a personal note, *thank you, Melissa* for truly being a beautiful winner in every possible way. In our years of working with pageants, you are among the most gracious & appreciative state winners we have had the pleasure to represent & we look forward to having you as part of our extended pageant 'family' for years to come! *Jim, Judy & staff*

Chapter 17

AMOR FATI

I returned home from competing at the Miss USA pageant in Baltimore, Maryland, with a great sense of peace and accomplishment. My lifelong dream of standing on that stage had come true, and more importantly, I made lasting friendships with the incredible women I had always admired. I also had a check for $1,000 from the then-Trump-owned Miss Universe Organization. The prize money was for winning the Miss Congeniality award.

I had a lot of bills to pay and not a lot of money. I spent most of my year as Miss Wisconsin USA volunteering, so I really could have used the $1,000. But I couldn't figure out anything worthy of spending that money on because of what it represented. It wasn't an award for being the most photogenic or having the best gown; it was for who I was, the kind of person I was, as awarded by my competitors. As I came from nothing, that check represented so many things, I couldn't bring myself to spend that money on anything. So I carried it around in my handbag for nearly a month.

As the reigning Miss Wisconsin USA, I was asked to appear at many community functions and charity events throughout the state. One afternoon in early May, I received a phone call from a nice woman who wanted me to speak on Mother's Day morning, before mass, to the women of her congregation. I was honored and happily accepted her invite.

Mother's Day morning came, and I dressed in my Sunday best with my Miss Wisconsin sash placed perfectly over my right shoulder; I followed the handwritten directions and made the journey to the event. As I neared my destination, things started to look very familiar. I drove past the address, and I immediately recognized the long concrete steps and the large doors of the church where I was scheduled to speak. My heart sank into the pit of my stomach as I realized that this was the same church where my family had received the tent twenty years earlier. I was in shock at the sight of the church, so I drove past it and parked two blocks away. I didn't want anyone to see me turn around if I decided I couldn't do it.

I had just returned from the Miss USA pageant a month before, and like the woman on the phone had asked, I was going to speak about my charitable work, what I had learned, and how it felt winning Miss Congeniality on national television—all pageant-related things. But when I got there, I knew I couldn't talk about those topics. They seemed shallow and insignificant compared to the meaning of what took place at that church and how it shaped the course of my life. Still sitting in my car, I was flooded with emotions. I didn't realize until then that I hadn't thought about that church very much, but now I was forced to.

As I started walking the two blocks to the church from where I had parked, many unresolved feelings washed over me, especially as I approached the steps, I could see myself sitting on the top step in those worn-out shoes. I could see my mother's tears. I could feel the rejection and the sadness like it was happening all over again. I could see exactly what it looked like, the pain of it, the memory—it was all right there.

While walking up the steps, I thought to myself, *How in the world am I going to be able to stand in front of this congregation and talk about my journey as Miss Wisconsin? How will I ignore the fact that this was the church that had an opportunity to save us and chose not to?* Instead, they gave my family the tent that ultimately placed us into foster care and the abuse that we suffered and the separation from our mother—all the pain and suffering that happened as result of that one moment. I hadn't stepped foot in that church since that day.

I reached for the door handle and said a silent prayer: *Please, God, reveal to me what this is all about. Why did you bring me back here? Please allow them to see you in me. Please give me the strength to speak to these women in a way that honors you.*

With the determination and guidance that could have only been gifted by the angels themselves, I took one step toward the light of spirit, and the spirit took ten steps on my behalf. Like a soldier, I reentered what I had once called God's house.

I was met by the sweetest lady who was very excited for me to speak. I think that she thought I was nervous, but there were no nerves. I was trying to keep my emotions in like trying to hold a beach ball underwater. I knew I couldn't speak about my journey as Miss Wisconsin. I had to tell a different story. But I had never told that story—not when I was competing for Miss Wisconsin and Miss USA, not when I was living in Los Angeles, not when I was in high school. I had never told anyone about my childhood. I didn't want pity. But I knew I had no choice at that point because the feelings were so strong. I was going to have to stand in front of the congregation and tell an entirely different story, a story I hadn't prepared.

As I was standing in front of the congregation where the priest usually stood, I was looking out at the pews that had been there for many, many decades—the same pews I had worshiped in as a small child and where we sat when my mother begged for help. Now I was an invited speaker, worthy of speaking to the congregation on their Mother's Day morning. The contrast was difficult to take in.

While I was gripping the microphone, the priest, a different one from when I was little, and the nuns were all sitting in the front row to hear my speech. I explained to the congregation that I had prepared to speak about my journey as Miss Wisconsin, but instead, I was going to tell them a story.

The church was quiet, and everyone was staring at me as I explained, "I'm going to tell you the story of a little girl who was born into severe poverty." I told of the early years of my life, of my mother being a Sunday school teacher, us attending church on Sundays, and how I thought that I was in God's house and it was a safe and loving place. I talked about how my mother volunteered, and even though we had very little, she would make care packages to be sent overseas. I explained how she often didn't know how she was going to feed us and how our electricity had been shut off, and we were evicted. I told how she dressed us in our finest hand-me-downs and how we followed her on foot to the church, how we sat in the pew and watched my mother cry and beg for help from the priest in the church where she had served for years.

At this point, people were starting to shift in the pews, and the priest and nuns in the front were looking uncomfortable; everyone was hanging on to my every word. A couple of older ladies yelled out, "Where was this church?" One lady shouted, "I want to write them a letter!" I was faced with a decision.

Do I tell them that it's the church I'm standing in? Just as I asked myself that question, the answer came to me, and I just blurted out the words: "It doesn't matter. The church itself does not matter." Then I went on to explain, "The truth is it was the church that saved me. If they would have helped my family by giving us a place to stay and food to eat, they would have saved the day, but I probably wouldn't be here, standing in front of you, speaking right now. I probably wouldn't have been Miss Wisconsin or have the kind of heart that I do, because those difficult times shaped who I was to become. It made me fight so much harder. It made me love that much stronger. It made me a giver, not a taker. It made the victory so much sweeter and my appreciation for it all. I never took one moment of it for granted. I never had to step on anyone to get a little bit taller. I always lifted people along the way. In doing so, I was able to make wonderful relationships with the women whom I had always dreamed of being in the presence of. I wasn't just one of them—I was their dear friend and sister in Christ."

It was at that moment, in front of that church, when God revealed everything to me. That tent wasn't a rejection from him or the church. It was a gift, the best gift he ever gave me, and what I had always seen as a disappointment, as a symbol of being unworthy, was really a perfectly planned blessing. That tent was made of gold, and I wouldn't trade it for anything in the world. I felt tremendous peace and appreciation. Unlike the moment we were given the tent, I now felt like God had welcomed me back into his house, and he was there waiting for my return.

My unplanned speech must have resonated with the congregation because suddenly, they stood up and were clapping. It was the longest standing ovation I had ever received. The priest who was sitting directly in front of me gently wiped a tear from his cheek. He asked me to please attend mass, which was to follow. He said he was moved by my beautiful testimony of redemption and what a lesson it was. He kindly thanked me over and over.

I agreed to stay. I sat between two families in what I thought was the same pew that I had sat in as a little girl. During the offering, when the baskets came out, the father of one of the families sitting next to me took a five-dollar bill from his wallet and placed it in the basket, then he handed the basket to me. I set it in my lap as I reached down and opened my handbag to see what I had to give, and there it was, the $1,000 I had received from the Trump-owned Miss Universe Organization for winning Miss Congeniality. Without even thinking, the money that I had been holding on to for weeks that nothing—not even overdue bills— could pry from me, I grabbed all of it and placed the ten hundred-dollar bills on top of the basket. I looked up and spoke to God, "Maybe today they won't have to turn anyone away."

I left the church and walked the two blocks back to my car. I felt a thousand pounds lighter. I had never realized that for twenty years, I had carried the weight of that moment as a five-year-old. What a heavy weight that was. I didn't even know it was there until it was gone. I was free. I finally knew what it was like to have peace. I knew what it felt like to truly forgive. I knew what it was like to be grateful for a past I thought was terrible. I had a new understanding and love of my fate. So I walked away changed forever.

It was God who put it on that woman's heart to invite me to speak at the church because he needed me to return to the place where I thought he had left me. What a beautiful gift he gave to me. That church never knew that I was talking about them, but I truly believe I wasn't the only one who was changed that day.

"I have swept away your offenses like a cloud, your sins like the morning mist. Return to me, for I have redeemed you."
Isaiah 44:22

Chapter 18

New Beginnings, Sad Endings

After my reign as Miss Wisconsin USA came to an end, my longtime boyfriend, whom I met while living on my own in Los Angeles, asked for my hand in marriage. Sergio and I were married on October 7, 2006, in a tiny, hundred-year-old chapel in Wisconsin. On that most beautiful fall day, surrounded by our close family and friends, we vowed, before God, for better, for worse, for richer, for poorer, in sickness and in health, to love and cherish until death do us part—not realizing we would soon be tested on each one of those promises.

Life as newlyweds wasn't much different for us. We were still inseparable, only now we were living together in our new home in Wisconsin. We bought a trilevel home that resembles the one where my dream was introduced as a child. Sergio was trying to adjust to life in the Midwest. I remember laughing to tears the first time I watched him attempt to remove snow from my car. He was outside in the freezing cold, armed with a towel and a spatula that he had taken from our kitchen, completely unaware that there was such a thing as an ice scraper. He was out there attacking the snow like a samurai warrior.

Sergio's biggest adjustment was the change of pace from a big city to a small Midwest town. In Los Angeles, if you want to survive in traffic, you must be an aggressive driver. Where I grew up, when you're at a stoplight, you politely wait for the car ahead of you to move when the light turns green, even if it means watching the green light come and go a few times. This was a foreign concept to Sergio. While sitting at a stoplight, Sergio had a two-second rule—you best be rolling forward when that green light appeared, or you were going to hear the blaring of his horn. For the first few months, he literally terrorized the kind folks on the streets of my hometown. I was so embarrassed to ride along with him.

While Sergio was adjusting to the simple life, I was adjusting to the role of a housewife. Cooking was not my strong point. While living in Los Angeles, my apartment didn't have a kitchen, let alone a stove, so I was off the hook. Our new home, of course, was equipped with all those things, and I wanted to impress my husband with nice home-cooked meals. When I didn't know what I was doing, I would improvise. One afternoon he returned from work early as I was preparing an Italian feast. I had no idea he was home. I was caught red-handed attempting to cut the Italian bread with a pair of scissors. I was snipping away at it when I heard him laughing out loud from behind me. I was afraid to use our new and very sharp knives, so I decided the scissors were a safer bet. Sergio put his arms around me and said in his spot-on Ricky Ricardo accent, "Luuucy, you have some 'splaining to do."

Cooking skills weren't the only area in which I was lacking. I couldn't keep a house plant alive for the life of me. Even the ones my mother brought over that were supposed to be "impossible" to kill were pronounced dead within a few weeks of being in my care. It was a running joke that had Sergio pondering my ability to handle the brood of little ones he was so eager for us to have.

Sergio came up with what he thought was a master plan. If he got me a puppy, my true mothering skills would be revealed. We rescued a five-week-old dachshund-terrier mixed puppy from a very bad situation. We named him Baron. On our way home, as I held Baron in my lap, wrapped in a warm towel, Sergio made it clear, "He's just going to be your dog." That was perfectly fine with me. I was in love with him from the first moment we made eye contact. It felt like we had an understanding—I was his mama, and he was my fur baby. That night, like a first-time mother, I didn't sleep a wink. Baron had to be bottle-fed and kept warm. He was sickly, and I was determined to nurse him to good health.

It didn't take long for Sergio to change his tune about Baron just being "my dog." The next day, we took him to the veterinarian, where they discovered that he had worms. After receiving the news, I looked over at Sergio; he was in tears and holding his stomach. He was clearly heartbroken and stated that he had a "sympathy bellyache" for Baron. It was clear that just overnight, Sergio had also fallen in love with the little pup too.

Baron changed our lives. We could no longer be selfish with our time. He fully depended on us. We took him everywhere including a cross-country road trip to visit Sergio's family in California. Baron sat on my lap for the entire ten-day journey. From the very beginning, he was my little fur baby. Sergio said that I passed his test with flying colors.

In early November 2007, just over a year after saying "I do," Sergio and I were having dinner with my mother and stepfather at their home. As I was sitting at my parents' dining room table, enjoying everyone's company, I began to feel funny. My vision was blurry, and everyone's words were mixing together. In a fog, I managed to muster enough strength to utter the words, "I think I'm going to—" And then I passed out. My limp body slumped over in my chair. Everyone was frantically trying to wake me up, but there was no response. My mother called 911 and explained what they had witnessed and begged for them to hurry up and help me. Sergio panicked and couldn't wait any longer, so he swooped me up and placed me in our SUV. Racing down the road, he passed the ambulance that was headed toward my parents' house.

When he pulled up to the hospital, there were people from the ER outside waiting for us. Obviously, I have no memory of those events. The last thing I knew, I was sitting at the table, feeling dizzy and weak. I remember opening my eyes as they were drawing blood from my arm.

Sergio was sitting next to me with his hand on mine. The doctor asked many questions: "Have you eaten today? Do you have any heart issues that you know about? Could you be pregnant?" He turned to Sergio: "Did she hit her head when she lost consciousness?"

Sergio explained, "She did eat today. We were just sitting down for dinner, and I don't think she has any heart issues. She works out five days a week. I don't think she's pregnant. We've been trying for a year with no luck, and no, she didn't hit her head."

The ER doctor reassured us that he was going to get answers about what was going on. As we waited for the blood test results, the ER doctor ordered a series of tests and scans. A young woman from the radiology department entered my room and explained to Sergio that she was taking me for some tests, and I would be back soon. As she was wheeling me down the long, cold hallway, I could hear the ER doctor's voice coming from behind us.

"Stop! Stop! Take her back to her room," he shouted. The woman turned my bed around and returned me to the room where Sergio and the doctor were waiting. The doctor explained,

"I have some good news and some bad news. The bad news is that you passed out, and that can be very scary. The good news is that you are going to be parents. You're pregnant! The blood test shows that you're very early in your pregnancy, maybe a week and a half or two weeks along."

Sergio and I were over the moon. This was the blessing we had been praying for. Tears of joy and gratitude were streaming down our faces as we held each other in that ER room. But through the joy, in the deepest part of my soul, there was that inner voice telling me something was wrong. For the first time in my life, I failed to follow to the small, still voice that had always guided me like a northern star—a decision that would cost me everything.

The ER doctor said that I should make an appointment with my ob-gyn. No further tests were taken at that time. To them, the positive pregnancy blood test was a good-enough answer as to why I had passed out. I was discharged, and we were sent on our way.

That evening Sergio and I shared the wonderful news with our parents. His father, mother, and brother cheered with excitement through the speakerphone from Los Angeles. The news of their first grandchild was an answer to their prayers. I saved the final call for two very special people. My childhood foster parents, Calvin and Joyce Martin, had attended our wedding a year earlier and were very much a part of my adult life. Joyce answered in her typical loving voice, "Hello, sweet Melissa."

"Good evening, Joyce. Sergio is sitting here with me, and we have something to share with you." I didn't even get the words out, and she was hollering for Cal.

"We're going to have another grandbaby!" It was a beautiful moment followed by a conversation that will stay etched in my heart for eternity.

"Melissa, do you remember the promise I made to you when you were a little girl, on the day you left our home to live with your father?" Joyce asked. Of course, I had remembered. How could I forget?

"Yes, I do," I replied. "You promised that you'd always be with me."

She said, "I want you to listen very closely to what I am about to say just like you did back then. God didn't choose me to bring you into this world, but I love you as such. My promise to always be with you remains, but I want to add to it. I never go to the hospital when a baby is being born. I like to visit after the fact, but I promise you that I will be in that room on the day you give birth to your precious little angel. I won't miss it for anything. I'll be there no matter what." Joyce's words that evening left me feeling so special. She always had a way of making me feel that way, but the fact that she promised to be by my side in the delivery room when it wasn't her MO reminded me of my place in her heart.

The first thing the following morning, just like the ER doctor suggested, I scheduled an appointment with my ob-gyn. A few days later, during my appointment, another blood test confirmed that we were indeed expecting. He also gave us our due date, July 26, 2008. I explained to him at that time about my scary trip to the ER and my dizzy spells ever since. He reassured Sergio and me that everything was looking fine. Wanting to believe only the best, I once again chose to silence the inner voice that was telling me different.

I was in the best shape of my life, working out five days a week and feeling better than ever, up until passing out at my parents' house. Each day after our confirmed pregnancy, I was physically feeling worse. I was extremely dizzy; looking down was nearly impossible. I had to hold on to something such as a countertop just to feel secure walking through my home. My vision was altered, with little floating dots everywhere. My headaches were so severe, I had to wear my sunglasses, even indoors. I went to every scheduled doctor's appointment and each time explained my symptoms and concerns. My doctor's response remained the same: "It's your first pregnancy, you look great, baby looks great. You're fine."

I remember sitting in the waiting room before my doctor's appointments. I would watch other expectant mothers, some of which appeared to be in their final trimester, and they would have a baby on their hip and a toddler running around the room. As they chased after their little ones, with their bellies so big, they could hardly see their feet, I wondered to myself, *How in the world are they able to do that? I'm not even showing yet, and I'm having a difficult time sitting upright in my chair.*

I had always been healthy. Besides having my gallbladder removed years earlier, I had never been hospitalized for anything. Sergio and I had complete trust in my doctor. If he said I was A-OK, we had every reason to believe him. It never crossed our minds to get a second opinion. Plus he was right—I had never been pregnant before. How was I supposed to know? Maybe I was just a wimp.

It was Christmastime and around eight weeks into my pregnancy when Sergio's family came to visit us from California. I put tremendous pressure on myself to impress my new in-laws. Unfortunately, my body couldn't keep up with my wishes to put on the perfect Christmas display. I tried so hard to push through, wanting so badly to make my wonderful mother-in-law proud of the woman her son chose to spend the rest of his life with and the future mother of her grandchild. My heart broke when I heard her explaining to Sergio about how hard she worked during her pregnancy, cleaning houses all the way up until her due date. I was just in my first trimester, stuck in a body that felt weak and unfamiliar to me.

On Christmas morning, Sergio and I gathered around the tree with his family and unwrapped our gifts. My spirit was aglow with thoughts of the next Christmas, when we would be celebrating the birth of Christ with our new baby.

After our holiday celebration, Sergio helped me up to our room so I could lie down. Shortly after resting my eyes, I heard the phone ringing. Sergio was busy putting something together downstairs and couldn't hear it, so the answering machine picked up.

"Hi, Sergio. This is Cal. Could you please call me back as soon as possible? Thank you." I heard the message perfectly from my bedroom. I thought it was a little strange that Cal was calling to only speak with Sergio; that had never happened before. It also struck me as odd that Cal didn't say "Merry Christmas." Spending Christmas with Cal and Joyce Martin when I was a little girl was one of my most treasured memories.

A moment later, the phone rang again. This time it was my mother leaving a message: "Sergio, it's Micky. Please call me."

As I sat up in bed, I thought, *What in the world is going on? Why are my loved ones blowing up our phone, looking for Sergio?* The phone rang again. I thought, *Okay, that's it!* I carefully made my way to the nearest phone.

"Where is Sergio? I need to talk to him," my mother demanded.

"What is going on? Why is everyone calling for him?" I questioned. At this point, Sergio had entered the room, totally unaware of the missed phone calls.

My mother was persistent: "Is Sergio near you?"

"Yes, he just walked in," I answered. Her voice started to crack.

"Melissa, Cal just called me. He wanted to speak with Sergio because he's worried about you being pregnant and hearing the news."

"What news? Please tell me what's going on," I begged. My mother paused for a moment and then forced out the words.

"Cal and Joyce were in an accident on their way home from mass. Cal just has a few cuts and bruises, but Joyce didn't make it. She passed away. She's gone."

The phone slipped from my hand and fell to the floor. Sergio grabbed me as my knees went weak. I couldn't catch my breath. It felt like I had the wind knocked out of me.

"No! No! No!" I cried out in disbelief. She was a mother to me. She saved my siblings and me when we were little. Now I was about to be a mother myself. I was going to need her more than ever. How could God take her away on Christmas Day? She promised she would always be with me. She promised that no matter what, she would be in the delivery room when I gave birth. She promised! How could this be happening?

Joyce Martin, liturgist, dies in accident Dec. 25

KAUKAUNA -- Joyce Martin, liturgy and music coordinator at Holy Spirit Parish, Kimberly/Darboy, died Dec. 25 in a traffic accident.

It has been said that where there is grief, there is love. This is true, and mine was so deep that the days leading up to Joyce's funeral are a blur. I was just simply going through the motions. Cal decided that she should have all women pallbearers. He wanted me to be the one standing directly in front of the casket. He knew that I was struggling with my health, so he asked that I just lay my hand on the casket and lead her out of the church and to the hearse. I was more than honored to do so. Once again, I found myself leaning on Joyce for the strength I needed to make it through. Even in death, she was the one holding me up.

It was always clear that Joyce Martin had a profound impact on my life. It never went overlooked or unappreciated by my family or me. But it wasn't until her funeral that I realized we were just one of the thousands of lives that she touched. I had never seen anything like it and probably never will again. The large Catholic church that she and Cal took us to as youngsters living in their home was overflowing with folks who wanted to pay their respects. There wasn't one empty seat; from the floor to the balcony, it was standing room only, with a line of people outside, hundreds deep, wrapped around the block. There were five priests, a bishop, and a full choir. The service was being recorded for other congregations, from Chicago all the way to Italy. My entire family was in attendance, including my parents. I was seated in the front of the church; behind me were a warden and a whole row of inmates in shackles whom Joyce had ministered to in prison. Every walk of life, every soul was represented in that church, all brought together to celebrate the remarkable spirit that was Joyce.

What was revealed that day, in testimony after testimony, was that each one of us thought we were the most special person to Joyce. She was always present, appearing in each of our lives when we needed her the most. How was it humanly possible for her to be in all those places, in all those moments of need? Somehow she had infinite time for others. One of the priests mentioned the word *saint* in front of her name, and we all agreed that it fit perfectly. If anyone was worthy, it was her. She was the answer to every prayer that I prayed as a child. Her role and timing in my life reconfirmed my faith in God and preserved my innocence. Every decision that directed me on the path to success, self-love, and righteousness was a result of the light that she shone upon me. I was saved by God's amazing grace, his glory reviled through his faithful servant, an earth angel, Joyce. It was very fitting that he called her home on Christmas Day, a great reminder of what a gift she was and how blessed we were to have her. Once again it was a time to rejoice.

With each passing week of my pregnancy, the struggle to do daily tasks became increasingly difficult. I couldn't stand too long over the sink to brush my teeth without having to sit down. I couldn't stand in a warm shower for more than a few minutes. Our new trilevel home that I loved so much became a nightmare. I started doubting my own strength.

Why can't I do the things that other pregnant women can? I kept thinking to myself. *Just pull it together, Melissa!*

Sergio and I decided that we didn't want to know the sex of our baby until birth. There are very few true surprises with today's technology, and we were committed to being prepared either way. Since we had two spare bedrooms next to ours, Sergio went to work getting them "baby ready." Sergio believed with all his heart that we were having a girl, so he turned the larger of the two rooms into a princess nursery complete with pink carpeting and pink walls. It looked like Shelby's wedding scene in *Steel*

Magnolias, decorated floor to ceiling in blush and bashful. He assumed any daughter of mine would love it, considering pink is my signature color. The other much smaller room had baby-blue carpet and baby-blue walls just in case his prediction was wrong.

I, on the other hand, believed with all my heart that I was carrying a boy (only a boy could give a girl this much trouble), so much so that I offered up a deal with Sergio: "If it's a girl, you can name her, but if it's a boy, I get to choose his name." Sergio confidently agreed. He would name our daughter after his beloved grandmother Anastacia. I had decided on my son's name long before that moment, when I was a little girl playing house, pretending to be Jackie Kennedy. If I ever had a son, I would name him after somebody who was smart, handsome, charismatic, and a great leader. His name would be Jack, after our thirty-fifth U.S. president.

Preparing for our baby should have been one of the most joyous times of my life. My heart and soul were overflowing with love for my unborn child, but physically I felt like I was dying. I had always thought of myself as a tough cookie, but this pregnancy was literally bringing me to my knees. As someone who never complained a day in my life about my health, it should have been a red flag to my physician that I was in crisis. I was calling my doctor and nurse hotlines frequently for help with my symptoms of severe headaches, blurry vision, nausea, fatigue, heart palpitations, and dizziness while standing. In one of those phone calls, I stated that I would bring a sleeping bag and sleep in the waiting room until somebody agreed to help me. I was scared and desperate.

It was clear that Sergio was extremely concerned about my failing health but also that he didn't know where to turn. For his entire life, he was as healthy as a horse. He only saw a doctor as a child for mandatory checkups. As an adult, he didn't even have a primary care physician. My doctor was telling us that I was fine, and Sergio trusted his expert opinion. Call it naivety or denial, but he was of the mind-set "Doctor knows best." He would assist me with my appointments, where the nurse would have to hold me up on the scale just to check my weight. She appeared worried during my later visits. I don't know what took place behind closed doors, but on one occasion, she strongly expressed her concerns to the doctor in my presence. Again he explained, "This is your first pregnancy, you look great, baby looks great. You're fine."

During my third trimester, in addition to everything else, I was experiencing severe drops in blood sugar, also known as hypoglycemia. Sergio noticed that I was a little shaky and offered to pick me up an ice cream cone. It was a sunny day in June, and I had only been out and about for doctor's visits, so I decided to ride along on the short trip to the drive-through. As Sergio was paying at the window, his cell phone rang. He handed me the ice cream, and at the same time, my cell phone, which was in my lap, started ringing. It was Sergio's brother, Jose. I handed him the phone, and I heard Jose say, "Dad's dead."

Sergio held the phone to his ear with one hand and steered us out of the drive-through with the other. My jaw dropped at what I thought I had heard. With no expression on his face, Sergio calmly responded, "Okay, I'm driving right now. I'll call you back when I get home." Using his thumb, he flipped my phone shut and passed it back to me.

Assuming I had misunderstood Jose because Sergio seemed okay, I said, "Oh my goodness. I thought your brother said something awful. It scared me for a moment."

Sergio responded with his eyes on the road, "Yeah, my dad just died while taking a nap." Tears instantly came to the surface and rolled down my face. I reached over to put my arm around him. I was a mess, sobbing like a baby, but Sergio seemed calm, almost unaffected. I thought maybe he was in shock.

When we returned home, he called Jose back. His brother explained how they found his father in bed, dead. Justino appeared healthy. He was only in his late fifties and rode his bike every day to work and everywhere in the California sun. He had a heart attack and died, just like that, six weeks before the expected due date of his first grandchild.

Sergio's parents had been married for nearly forty years. The news was tragic and heartbreaking to all. Sergio said he wasn't comfortable leaving to attend his father's funeral this late in my pregnancy with my increasing health problems, but I insisted that he go. He finally agreed to a quick twenty-four-hour trip to attend the showing. He would miss the funeral. The next morning, Sergio boarded a plane for Los Angeles to bid a final farewell. His blasé response to the untimely death of his father was a concerning eye-opener for me, a clear indication of how he would cope with tragedy in the future.

While Sergio was boarding a plane headed for home, my father and his wife showed up at my front door with the sad news that his mother, my grandmother Carol, had passed away. When I was a teenager, my grandmother Carol gave me the most beautiful pair of emerald earrings. Emerald is my birthstone, and the earrings were the first real jewelry I ever owned. When she heard the news that Sergio and I were expecting, she had a beautiful pink-and-blue blanket knitted for our baby-to-be. She would never get to see our child wrapped in it—well, at least not from this side of heaven. I lost three loved ones in the course of six months.

My failing health continued to fall on deaf ears. Again, I had never been pregnant before, so when my doctor would tell me that I was fine, I would think that something was wrong with me. I always thought of myself as being a pretty tough cookie, but maybe I wasn't. How did other women make it look so easy?

As I inched closer to my due date, I needed assistance to use the restroom. At times it was difficult to lift my head. My once-healthy body was no more. I had no reference to what death felt like, but I thought this had to be it; and I was right, I was dying.

Like Job in the Bible, God had blessed me beyond measure. Was I only a faithful servant to God because he turned my life around and blessed me abundantly? How would I respond to losing it all? Would I praise him in unimaginable suffering? Would I continue to exhibit hope, patience, and perseverance? Would I bare grief and unrelieved misery with amazing submission? Would I cherish the worth of God above all else, including my health, or would I waver?

Chapter 19

AN ANGEL IN THE ROOM

On July 10, 2008, sixteen days before my due date, my severe headache and dizziness were making it nearly impossible to get ready for my routine doctor's appointment. As usual, I gave it my all, but this time, I didn't make it. I passed out. Sergio found me lying on the floor, and I was rushed to the hospital. Upon arrival, my blood pressure was 200/129. When my doctor entered the room, I once again pleaded with him, "I think I'm dying. Please help me." He agreed and finally ordered necessary blood tests. The lab tech came into the room and drew numerous vials of blood. My doctor instructed me to stay lying down on my side. For the first time, the man who had failed to hear me or even order simple tests had a look of concern in his eyes as he exited the room. Sergio was as quiet as a mouse while we waited for the results.

Sometime later my doctor reentered the room, but he didn't look the same. His usual rosy cheeks were now chalk white, the same color as the bedsheets. His nearly perfect posture was now slumped forward as if he was shrinking. His confident, slightly arrogant demeanor appeared meek and uncertain.

He sat down on his stool and slowly rolled over to the bed where I was still lying on my side as he earlier instructed. He glanced at Sergio and then back at me. He took in a deep breath and exhaled with enough force to blow out a candle. Then in a mild voice, he explained, the blood tests revealed I was suffering from a rare life-threatening condition called HELLP syndrome. HELLP stands for hemolysis (breakdown of red blood cells), elevated liver enzymes (liver function), and low platelet counts (platelets help to clot blood). In my case, it was caused by undiagnosed and untreated preeclampsia. Women with HELLP syndrome can die very easily. Mine was so severe, I was in a hypertensive crisis along with liver and kidney failure, and my blood was the consistency of water.

The doctor further explained that he was going to induce my labor and keep me on a constant drip of anti-seizure medication because my blood pressure was so high, I was at risk of having a stroke. He explained that he couldn't perform a C-section because of my low platelet count; I would bleed to death if they tried to cut me open. I would have to deliver naturally while my organs were failing.

Through my tears, I cried out, "But I was telling you that I wasn't okay. I went my whole life not being hospitalized, not being sick. I always took very good care of myself. I ate healthily and worked out frequently, and suddenly when I got pregnant, I couldn't do anything. So as someone who never complained a day in my life about my health, why wasn't that a red flag to you? When I begged you over and over to please help me, why didn't you hear me? Why?"

With his eyes focused down at his shoes, he responded, "I couldn't see it. I couldn't see past the way you look. You look great. You only gained 26 pounds throughout your pregnancy, not the massive water-retention weight, up to 100 pounds, usually associated with severe preeclampsia and HELLP syndrome. Your blood tests show that you are now in liver and kidney failure. The whites of your eyes should be pure yellow, but they're not. They're bright white. I couldn't see it! I couldn't see it!" he repeated.

He couldn't see it on the outside, so he failed to hear me or order any tests. I was treated like a dramatic first-time pregnant woman who didn't know how to cope with the changes to my body. But he was so wrong. I struggled greatly every day, week, and month of my pregnancy. My concerns and cries for help repeatedly fell on deaf ears. I beat myself up for being a wimp. I silenced the spiritual guide of my inner voice and listened to an outside opinion. I trusted a white lab coat instead of the shoulder taps from God.

I was wheeled to a labor and delivery room, where they started me on Pitocin to induce my labor and very high doses of anti-seizure medication. The nurses placed a pillow underneath my bottom to help with blood pressure. They said I would have to remain in the same position, lying down for the entire labor and delivery. I wouldn't be able to use my body to help things along. I was instructed not to move.

My hospital room quickly filled up with nurses and staff. By this time my mother had arrived. She immediately joined me at my bedside and was overcome with emotion. I was unable to lift my head, so I let it fall slightly toward my left shoulder to prevent choking on my vomit. My mother grabbed a plastic container and held it underneath my chin. The nurse stopped counting after twenty purges; at that point, I had nothing left inside of me. Throughout the room, the presence of fear was tangible. In the midst of the piercing sounds of alarms, the urgency of shuffling feet, and the swooshing of my baby's strong heartbeat, from the deepest part of my soul, I humbly spoke to God. I praised him for blessing me with the twenty-nine incredible years of life, for testing me, using me, and forgiving me. I asked that he place a hand of protection over my child.

"It's okay if you need to call me home, but please be with my child."

I remember following my husband and my mother with my eyes as they were called out of the delivery room. In the hallway, the doctor explained to them that I might not make it through this natural birth. At the time, I didn't know exactly what information they were receiving, but I knew it was serious. A moment later, I heard an animallike sound coming from my mother. I had never heard anything like it. It was the sound of excruciating pain coming from the depths of one's soul. The tortured scream was followed by the words, "You are killing her! You are killing my daughter!" I wanted so badly to comfort her but couldn't.

When Sergio and my mother re-entered the room, I was staring at them, trying to get them to look me in the eye. It was at that moment that I realized, I wasn't the only one who was dying. They wouldn't make eye contact with me. My mother was looking down at the ground, looking side to side, and at one point looking through her purse frantically like she didn't even know what she was searching for, anything to not look at me because it was too painful.

I stared at Sergio, desperately wanting him to look back at me, but he was gone. He was physically there next to me, but it was like looking at a stranger in the room. There was no life in him at all, no spirit, just a shell of a human being. That was the last time I saw Sergio, not physically but every part of him beneath the skin. That old feeling of abandonment was back to pay me a visit, brought to the surface by my husband.

I was surrounded by people but felt very much alone. As I scanned the room, desperately seeking comfort and reassurance through eye contact, I noticed a small tarnished cross on the wall of the old Catholic hospital. It obviously had been there all along, probably for over fifty years, but this was the first time I noticed it. With my eyes focused on the cross, I couldn't help but think of Joyce. She had promised me that she was going to be there, and I needed her more than ever. My mother and Sergio had checked out, and I felt like she wouldn't have. In my head, with all my heart and soul, I spoke to her, "Joyce, you promised that you'd never leave me, but I'm asking you to shift that promise. You don't need to watch over me anymore. Instead please be with my unborn child. Please keep him or her safe from harm. You promised me that you'd be here in this moment, and I believe you are. Please take your eyes off me now and focus on my little one. This is all I ask."

While talking to Joyce in heaven, I heard a familiar voice at my feet. It was my sister and lifelong protector, Michelle. My mother had called her and my father after receiving the devastating news from the doctor in the hallway. My father was in the waiting room, a few doors down, and as usual, Michelle was demanding answers and holding everyone accountable.

As the sunlight faded from the third-floor window in room 388, I thought to myself, *Is this my last sunset? I wish I would have taken time to appreciate them more. I wish I wouldn't have overlooked the beauty of a day well lived and the anticipation of a new one on the horizon.* I thought about all the sunsets that my child would experience. I prayed that he or she wouldn't take a single one for granted, and I promised, if I was blessed with more, I wouldn't either.

It was now the middle of the night, and I was in full fight. I could feel a separation between my spirit and physical being. It was like a war between the two. My body was failing, so I was counting on my spirit for survival. As my contractions were increasing and becoming more intense, something happened. I felt a sudden, very severe pain in my head, as if I was being stabbed there. At the same time, my reflexes went haywire. My arms and legs were making sharp, forceful movements beyond my control; for some reason, they were worse on my right side. My doctor immediately took notice and called on the staff in the room to help hold me in place. It's documented in my medical records that during this time, I stated, "I think something happened to my brain," and unfortunately, those words would prove to be right.

That was the longest, most horrific night of my life. The physical and emotional pain was indescribable. It was also taking a toll on everyone in the room, including the doctor who had dismissed my struggles during my pregnancy. He made a plea to his colleague, "This woman is dying, and she is suffering. Normally we wouldn't give an epidural to someone with such low blood platelets, but we should do it." The anesthesiologist agreed. He marked a spot on my back and skipped the usual step of numbing the area because of my allergy to numbing medications, including lidocaine. I felt every bit of him inserting the epidural. Unfortunately, I think my water-like blood interfered with its effectiveness. I would have to continue to endure natural labor without an intervention.

There was a young nurse practitioner in the room that was visibly shaken. She was the only person making eye contact with me, and I could see the fear in her eyes. The people I love the most couldn't look at me. They were focused on my unborn baby, which was the answer to my prayer that day, when I prayed, "Just be with my child."

Twenty-five hours after being induced, at 4:07 p.m. on July 11, 2008, I gave birth to a baby boy. I never got to hold him. They didn't place him on my chest because of my failing health. I couldn't see him, but I could hear the beautiful, strong sound of his cry. Sergio said, "Mama, you have a son." From across the room, I heard a nurse announce, "He weighs seven pounds, fourteen ounces and measures twenty-two inches long." The doctor asked her to say that again as he was quickly sewing me up and trying to stop the bleeding. He couldn't believe his ears because he was expecting my baby to be less than six pounds. The nurse asked Sergio if we had a name for him.

He responded, "Yes, his name is Jack." I had won the wager with Sergio regarding the gender. My gut instinct was correct; I had been carrying a baby boy. His name would be Jack after our thirty-fifth U.S. president, John F. Kennedy.

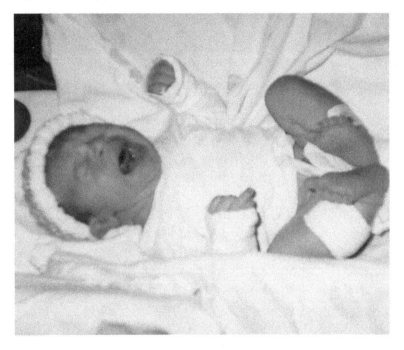

Jack was perfect, seemingly unfazed by the trauma I was going through. Joyce had kept her promise after all. I believe with my whole heart that she made that promise knowing that, without a doubt, she would be in that room, not in the physical form but in spirit. Once again, she kept her word. Her presence was palpable. Joyce was an Angel to me as a little girl, and now she could be that for my little boy. I wouldn't doubt if she played a role in sending his sweet soul to me as well, like he was handpicked by heaven's best to be my son and to give me the superpowers to fight on.

By the grace of God, Jack was healthy and cleared to go home a couple of days later.

Most often, the definitive treatment for women with HELLP syndrome is the delivery of their baby. Sadly, that wouldn't be the case for me. The days after giving birth to Jack were horrendous. I still couldn't move. I remember always feeling wet and sticky. I had a pillow underneath me all the time to help with my blood pressure, and when they'd remove the pillow, you could ring it out; it was so wet with blood. Even days after delivery, I was still losing a lot of blood because my platelet count was so low, there was no clotting. My blood pressure remained dangerously high. I was on two hundred milligrams of Labetalol (beta-blockers) per day and toxic levels of anti-seizure medication. There was no relief from the severe head pain and vomiting, and my reflexes still had a mind of their own. I was in such bad shape, my body was failing, and my voice was fading. I knew I was going to die if I stayed there.

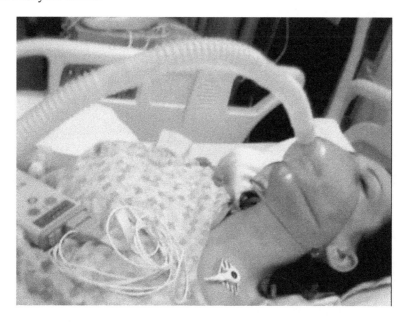

Chapter 20

FOR THE BENEFIT OF JACK

After giving birth to Jack, my health condition didn't improve; it rapidly declined. New, unfamiliar, and complicated issues presented themselves. The insufficient expertise of my health care providers proved to be a major problem. God's divine intervention showed up in the form of a new doctor. He was very concerned and perplexed by my symptoms that were now beyond HELLP syndrome. He couldn't understand why I hadn't been transferred to a better-equipped hospital before or directly after giving birth. He immediately arranged for me to be seen by a specialist at a hospital in Milwaukee, Wisconsin.

Upon arrival at the hospital in Milwaukee, I was examined by a neurologist who specialized in rare conditions. His appearance seemed straight out of a classic television show. He was a tall, lean man with a perfect side part in his hair. His clothes appeared tailor fit, topped off with a plaid-patterned bow tie. His leather shoes had obviously been repaired with new soles, and he spoke in a very heavy accent. He carried a vintage leather medical saddlebag that split open at the top. His lips were pressed firmly together as he witnessed my uncontrollable reflexes and extreme fluctuation in blood pressure and heart rate.

During his examination, my resting heart rate, lying down, was 126 bpm. When he positioned me upright, my heart rate would skyrocket near 200 bpm, and at the same time, my blood pressure would plummet, making it nearly impossible to stand without losing consciousness. Visibly distraught, the neurologist asked why it took so long for me to get proper medical attention. He ordered blood work—twenty-four vials to be exact—and called on a colleague from cardiology. They spent hours running tests and examining me from head to toe. I was thankful to finally be in the hands of a specialist who was very thorough.

The unique neurologist humbly explained that although I was now at one of the best hospitals in the state, my medical situation was beyond even their level of expertise. I would need to be transferred four hours away to the Mayo Clinic in Rochester, Minnesota. I knew exactly where I was headed. It was the same world-renowned medical facility where my grandmother Nancy was treated for a rare brain tumor many years earlier.

The Mayo Clinic in Rochester, Minnesota, is considered the very best, having treated presidents of the United States and dignitaries from all around the world. Different from any other hospital you've ever seen, it's like a city within itself, measuring three times larger than the Mall of America. It's equipped with underground access from clinic to clinic and a list of amenities too long to mention. The incredible structure compliments their astounding personalized care. God had sent me to a place that housed the most remarkable minds on earth. I prayed that they would hold the knowledge regarding my peculiar condition and ultimately save my life.

At the Mayo Clinic, I was blessed to be in the care of an amazing team led by a world-renowned professor of neuroscience known for being a pioneer in his field. In addition to the brilliant professor of neurology, the team consisted of specialists in cardiology, endocrinology, and gastroenterology, a medical dream team all working together on my behalf.

More concerned with the care of my son than myself, in place of visitors, I rallied the closest, most trusted people in my life— Sergio, my mother, and my sister, Michelle—to care for Jack back at home. The only thing more painful than my circumstances was the heartache of missing my sweet boy. I was desperate and would do anything for more time with him.

I would undergo many grueling tests; every heartbeat was recorded, every drop of urine was collected, every blood pressure and blood sugar change were noted, every morsel of food eaten was counted, and every ounce of vomit was measured. Every function of my body was literally under a microscope.

After a week of me enduring the nonstop medical tests, one after another, the team of specialists came into the room to talk with me. This was it, my diagnosis was determined and written somewhere on the computer screen in front of the professor. In a kind and compassionate manner, he explained that I was suffering from autonomic failure, dysautonomia, and hyperadrenergic POTS (postural orthostatic tachycardia syndrome). It turns out I was correct when I said, "Something happened to my brain," while giving birth to Jack.

The professor stated that it started in the first trimester of pregnancy, complicated by preeclampsia, which graduated to HELLP syndrome. The severe trauma and prolonged suffering contributed to the part of my brain that controls the autonomic nervous system to shut off like a light switch. Sadly, there is no way to manipulate the brain to tell it how to do its job. They can remove tumors from the brain and do lots of amazing things, but they can't tell it how to work.

The autonomic nervous system controls the body functions not consciously directed (hence the prefix *auto-*). In other words, it's the part of our brain that controls all automatic functions that we don't think about, such as breathing, heart rate, blood pressure, body temperature, pupil dilation, digestive processes, and most vital organs. Like a defense mechanism, it shut off when my body was shutting down. I was left with an overactive sympathetic nervous system, the system that activates what is often termed the fight-or-flight response. My overactive or (hyperadrenergic) state was now overcompensating and in control of my survival.

My sympathetic overactivity and orthostatic intolerance were characterized by symptoms of light-headedness and syncope, blood pooling in my abdomen and feet, severe tachycardia and palpitations (equivalent to running on a treadmill at all times), nausea and vomiting (rapid gastric emptying), hypovolemia, and dehydration. My body could not retain sodium when ingested orally. In a twenty-four-hour urine collection, my sodium levels should be 140, ideally 170 mmol; mine repeatedly came back dangerously low, under 17 mmol. I was at risk of going into hypovolemic shock. I would need two liters of sodium chloride administered intravenously each day moving forward. Just imagine functioning solely on adrenaline while unable to adjust to the pull of gravity. You can't!

The epidural that I received during labor wasn't effective and caused more harm than good. For months while undergoing countless tests and procedures, I was suffering from an excruciating headache. It was indescribable. Out of the blue, one of the specialists said he couldn't imagine that they would have given me an epidural during my labor because I had such low blood platelets. He asked, "Can you tell me if that happened or not?"

I answered, "Yes, they did, but it didn't work."

They then discovered that the hole hadn't healed, and I was leaking cerebral spinal fluid into my brain stem; it was sitting there like a water balloon. He explained, "We need to patch the hole, but the problem is there is no medical record of you receiving an epidural." Anytime anyone gets an epidural, there is a medical form with an outline of a body. They put an X at the exact site where they make the hole for the epidural so that if anything goes wrong, physicians can go right to that spot. He explained that he didn't know where the hole was, and because it had been months, he couldn't see the site from the outside, so he would have to patch my entire spine with my own blood and hope that it finds the hole and clots it.

For the procedure, I had to lie on my stomach. They took blood from my arm in a long tube and pushed it through my entire spinal cord, hoping my own blood would clot the hole, wherever it was. Because I am allergic to numbing medications, I felt every bit of the six-inch needle going into the bottom of my spine and sitting there. I was instructed not to move a muscle, so I kept my head faced down in a pillow and allowed it to soak up my tears. The pressure of my spine receiving all the blood felt like it was going to explode back there. But finally, it did its job; my own blood healed the hole in my spine.

After months of receiving care at the Mayo Clinic, bizarre tests and painful poking and prodding became a way of life. It was a far cry from my once-healthy body that not long before had competed on the Miss USA stage. This was my new reality; with no cure in sight and my heart now in the condition of an elderly woman, I had nowhere to turn but to God. I didn't have a choice in what happened to me, but I had a choice in how I saw it and how I received it. God's plans for my life are greater than any illness. My body is only temporary, but my spirit lives on forever. I made a promise to myself, *This will not get the best of me. The best of me belongs to that precious baby boy.*

Trapped in a world that was foreign to me, I was physically unable to do the things I loved and the things I'd always dreamed of. My moments with Jack weren't even close to what I had envisioned motherhood would be like. I never had the privilege of walking the floor with him or the honor of pushing him in a stroller on a sunny day. I couldn't run after him at the park, but anybody could do those things that I couldn't.

It was what I could do that ended up holding the most value. There was a silver lining to the debilitating illness that slowed me down. It forced me to be still and present in the moment. It was a huge contrast from the dream chaser and go-getter I had always been, but it proved to be exactly what Jack needed. He didn't see my shortcomings. He thrived from our endless snuggles, giggles, hand-holding, storytelling, tear wiping, singing, kissing, and hugging moments. I was able to fill his spirit with affirmations and life lessons with no distractions or demands from the outside world. Our connection was rooted from the deepest part of our souls, resulting in a bond that is irreplaceable. My life wasn't how I pictured it would be as a mother; it was better because it was perfectly orchestrated by God for the benefit of Jack.

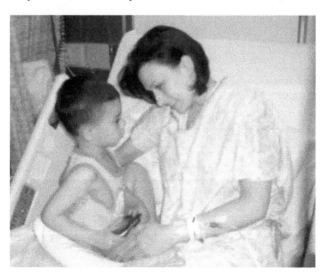

Chapter 21

My Purpose

J ack and I have a special connection. I can read him like a book. But other people were having a more difficult time understanding what Jack was wanting or needing. He never went to daycare or to a babysitter. He just had Sergio, me, my sister, and my mother caring for him. Jack has a cousin who is ten days older, and I could see that there was a difference in the way they communicated and how they expressed their wants and needs. At a wellness check, Jack's pediatrician suggested it might be because Jack wasn't around any other kiddos; he was only around adults, so maybe he socially wasn't learning like he should from other children. Maybe he didn't have to express himself because we were always at his beck and call. I admit, I kept him in a bubble out of fear that anything would happen to him, recognizing how precious life was, as I was not able to get a handle on my own failing health.

Sergio and I were first-time parents, so I wanted to know if his differences were because I was keeping him in that adult bubble or if there was something else going on. After further conversations with his wonderful pediatrician, he suggested that we take him to a children's hospital and meet with a physician to make sure that there wasn't something else we should be aware of.

There was something special about my sweet Jack. Sergio and I made the journey to a children's hospital in hopes of learning more regarding just how special he was. Jack was eighteen months old, and I was just recovering from a heart procedure, with an incurable illness, when we made this journey.

When we arrived, we were put into a room with a long couch and dozens of toys. Sergio and I noticed a two-way mirror on the back wall. We found it interesting that others may be looking in on our appointment. Ten or fifteen minutes later, a female doctor walked in and sat on the floor next to Jack as he was playing with a toy train. She was talking in a voice that wasn't gentle or kind; it seemed that she was trying to provoke him to see if he would have a fit or some sort of reaction. But that wasn't Jack. He had never thrown a temper tantrum. Jack wasn't having the difficulties of a typical almost two-year-old; he was very compliant. While visiting the public library for story time or the children's museum, when other little ones would throw fits, Jack would just stare at them like, "What's wrong with that child? Why are they acting like that?" He was never doing anything that we needed to correct, so there weren't many opportunities for us to teach.

The doctor still seemed to want to provoke him, holding on to his hands so he couldn't touch the toys. He allowed her to do it but looked terrified of her. He had always been in the loving arms of us, so I'd never seen that look on his face before. I was already feeling upset by her cold demeanor and lack of compassion. As a mother, I felt defensive and protective. I squeezed Sergio's hand as hard as I could, and before I could get a word out, she looked at us, and in a cold, matter-of-fact way, she spewed out the words, "Your son has autism. I knew it the moment I walked into the room. Yep, he's autistic."

Stunned that any physician would diagnose within minutes and recalling my own experience with the doctor who made a major diagnostic error, I asked her, "So what did you think of me when you walked into the room?"

She confidently replied, "You are probably in your late twenties or early thirties. You look like you take great care of yourself and are in good health."

I responded, "With all due respect, ma'am, you are wrong about me. I am fighting for my life, and you are wrong about my

Jack." Wanting to lift him to my chest but unable to because of my physical condition, I took him by his hand.

As we were exiting the room, she gently touched my arm and went on to explain, "Your son will never be capable of more than sitting in a circle and holding hands and maybe putting his own toys away. He will never attend public school and will need forty hours a week of in-home therapy."

I couldn't believe she was going to put my son in a box and put such low expectations on his life in a matter of minutes. I wondered, *What if I hadn't just gone through a horrible medical error myself? What if I hadn't had this knowledge when I was bringing Jack to her? Would I have blindly believed her?*

On our way out of the office, the receptionist stopped us and said, "You need to sign the medical release forms so we can send the diagnosis to Jack's pediatrician."

I whispered, "You need to shred that. I will not sign a release form. I'm not even going to say that I was here." I knew that physician was wrong about what my Jack would be capable of.

I asked God, "Why Jack?" *With everything that happened to me, to give him life, didn't I take a bullet for the both of us? Why wasn't my suffering enough? Why couldn't I protect him from this?*

Just as I cried out to the Lord, he spoke to my heart, "Jack is your purpose."

At that moment, everything became crystal clear. I was called to be Jack's mother. Without me, the lights would go out for him. I would need to enter Jack's world and allow him to be my earthly spirit guide.

It sums up what Jesus meant when he said, "Truly I tell you, unless you change and become like little children, you will never enter the kingdom of heaven." (Matthew 18:3

That physician's low expectations for Jack's life lit a fire in me to fight on as I had my whole life. But this was like pouring gasoline on it. I knew I had to be here for Jack and that no one could take my place. At that time, I was hoping and praying that I could just be here long enough to be in his memory. But now leaving him to face this big ol' world without me was not an option. We were in this together.

What I realized early on was that I wasn't going to be engaging with Jack in the typical way that you would with other kids. If Jack wanted to fidget with something—Jack loved to fidget with anything, like pieces of paper that he moved back and forth—rather than taking it away and replacing it with something more typical like building blocks, I would get a piece of paper and fidget with him. Instead of trying to pull him out of his comfort zone, I joined him there. That's where Jack was living, in that comfort zone. I essentially had to become autistic. I had to move into his world and live there. It didn't matter if I was hooked up to an IV or heart monitor; if Jack wanted to listen to the same song fifty times, we listened to the song together. If he wanted to read the same book over and over, we read it together. It was in those moments when Jack allowed me in, making eye contact with me and asking me a lot of questions. He would express all kinds of love by hugging and kissing me and holding my face in his hands. He was so engaged. There was no place I'd rather be than in Jack's world because that's where he was; it's where I heard the words "I love you, Mama."

I was afraid that if God took me home during this time, how would anyone else know how to do this? Everyone loved him so dearly, but it was his response to me that was working. I wasn't following any milestone chart or rule book; I was following the book of Jack. After joining him in his comfort zone for so long, I started introducing new things, and he allowed them in. He trusted me and slowly followed me out. I watched him see the light. We saw it together.

Jack far exceeded the modicum expectations of that physician. I am grateful that the good Lord gave me the wherewithal to not allow her to put a lid on the box she put him in. He is brilliant, demonstrating abilities that are in excess of what would be considered normal. His memory is extraordinary. His mind is like a filing cabinet—if he sees or hears something once, it's there forever. He has a unique gift of recalling events in his life by the date, day of the week, and time they occurred. He knows the exact distance to locations all around the world, like a human GPS. His accuracy will leave you speechless. He has wonderful relationships with his teachers and friends and a sense of humor that will make you belly laugh.

For Mother's Day, Jack and his classmates made cards at school to take home to their mothers. They were to make a complete sentence with "I love you because . . ." Most of the kiddos' responses were silly and sweet. For example, "I love you because you make my favorite food," or "I love you because you buy me toys." But it was how Jack finished the sentence that said it all: "I love you because you bring me to good places." Those words were so deep and meaningful because with my health struggles, I was never able to take him anywhere physically. He was talking about a state of being, not an actual place. That little Mother's Day card sits at my bedside and is my most treasured possession.

Glory be to God for placing me in this position. I was so driven, always chasing the next big dream to prove that I was going to be somebody, I wouldn't have known how to slow down. Being sick forced me to be still. I was fighting for my life, and I was Jack's mommy, and that was it. Everything I did was for him; he had all of me. My illness put me in an uncomfortable place. I didn't know what each day was going to bring, so I could only live in those moments with Jack. It was exhausting, beautiful, and rewarding. There are so many obvious blessings in this health crisis, and Jack is the best one.

> "And we know that in all things God works for the good of those who love him, who have been called according to his purpose." Romans 8:28

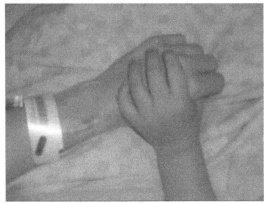

Chapter 22

A Blessing the Size of Texas

A brilliant professor of neuroscience said that I have one of the most complex cases of dysautonomia, hyperadrenergic POTS, and autonomic failure. There was no particular textbook on my case, so I chose to become one, volunteering my body for research studies. I no longer had a name; I was referred to as a number in a research lab. Desperate for a cure, I willingly underwent bizarre and strenuous tests that would start early in the morning and end at 5:00 p.m. for days on end.

I was put into sweatboxes naked because sweating is part of the autonomic nervous system, and they wanted to study how that pattern had failed. They covered my naked body in a yellow powder that would turn purple wherever I'd sweat. I would enter the box, which was almost like a coffin, then they would slowly increase the temperature until my body was overheated. The common places that are supposed to turn purple, like the forehead or armpits, didn't change color on me. The tests confirmed my inability to sweat even with an induced fever.

I underwent repeated tilt table tests where they would strap me to a table while I was hooked up to countless electrodes, then move the table from lying flat to a ninety-degree upright position. The tilt table test would confirm my body's inability to remain upright along with regulating blood pressure and heart rate. When I would lose consciousness, they would lower the bed back to a flat position and administer IV fluids. After the IV hydration, they would repeat the test, determining that I could stay upright longer with the increased blood volume from receiving liters of sodium chloride. I couldn't live without daily IV hydration. The problem was there was no end to this insight, and a person only has so many veins. I tried every medication known to man and even ones that weren't; experimental drugs that didn't even have names yet, I tried them. Unfortunately, nothing compared to the results of IV hydration; some of them even made things worse.

During this time, I lay low, not sharing my health struggles with the outside world. I was focused on fighting my way out of the illness that had taken residence within me. That's when a dear friend from sixteen years earlier literally flew back into my life, flying from her home in San Antonio, Texas, to Rochester, Minnesota, to be by my side. Her name is Kelly Hall, but I call her Tex, and she calls me Consin, for obvious reasons (Texas and Wisconsin). Tex and I have a friendship that is straight out of the movie *Fried Green Tomatoes*. We met in our early teens. She was tiny but tough and a great softball player, even becoming a coach after college. She is a tomboy and a beauty queen all wrapped in one. While her frame is petite, her personality is larger than life. Her distinct laugh followed by a snort gives her presence away every time. She was my Idgie, and I was her Ruth. There is nothing we wouldn't do for each other. It's quite possible that we were the only ones ever to fill the walls of the hospital's research lab with laughter. The good Lord had sent me a blessing the size of Texas. Kelly came back into my life when I needed her the most.

"Don't urge me to leave you or to turn back from you.
Where you go I will go, and where you stay I will stay.
Your people will be my people and your God my God."

Ruth 1:16

No matter how painful and grueling it was to be a human guinea pig in a research lab, I was beyond grateful for the insight I was receiving about my illness. I realized early on that they probably wouldn't find a cure from my body alone, but the information discovered was valuable to medical science, and maybe, just maybe, someone wouldn't have to suffer as bad as I was because I took one for the home team. That, in and of itself, was good enough for me.

With little to no funding for research or treatment for rare illnesses, the dysautonomia research department closed due to lack of funding. Funding goes to the disorders that affect more people, not medical mysteries that no one has ever heard of, like mine. Without coverage from my health insurance to continue care at the Mayo Clinic, I was now considered a pay-as-you-go patient. Sergio and I were buried past our eyeballs in medical bills. His wages were being garnished, and that wasn't making a dent in them. It wasn't like paying for a prior procedure; I needed constant, ongoing medical care. It would be impossible to catch up. Even if he worked until he was ninety years old, it wouldn't be enough. Between my ongoing medical issues and raising a child with special needs, our family was in a devastating financial crisis. I had no choice but to return to the hospital that my insurance would cover, back to where this nightmare began.

Chapter 23

A Gift Too Great to Receive

Having to return to the cold walls where my health crisis went overlooked was unspeakable. It's like your spirit returning to the scene of the accident where you died and forcing it to exist in that space.

The only upside to my return was that I was closer to home and my sweet Jack. My family was near, but their presence was not. I was lonelier than ever. After the birth of Jack, Sergio was completely withdrawn from me. I had to mourn the loss of us like a death. He directed all his love, affection, concern, and attention toward Jack, which was exactly where I prayed it would be, but for some reason, since the horrific events in the delivery room, he couldn't include me.

During their visits to the hospital, while Jack and I snuggled together in my hospital bed, Sergio would purposely take the seat closest to the door and farthest away from me. When I attempted to engage in conversation, Sergio would look down or in the opposite direction as if he couldn't hear me. I felt like I was in the movie *Ghost*, when Sam was trying to connect with Molly from the other side. I was trying to get Sergio's attention, but my presence seemed too painful for him. It appeared as if he had already said his goodbyes, and I was just a reminder of what used to be. We had been partners since I was nineteen years old, and now my existence was put away somewhere in his past. I was no longer the focus of his future; Jack was. Our little boy was now the love of our lives and the only link holding us together.

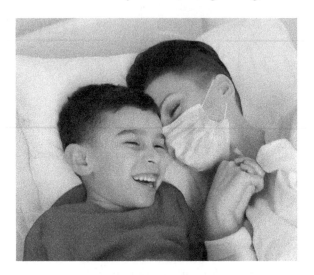

I tried to be understanding of Sergio's pain, acknowledging that I wasn't the only one hit by a train; he too was on the tracks that day. The difference was that I decided to crawl off and get help, and he remained lying there, allowing the train to continue running him over. I was going from specialist to specialist, undergoing procedure after procedure, and volunteering my body for research, essentially scratching and clawing at any opportunity that might save my life, and he wouldn't even talk to a therapist to save himself, let alone our marriage.

Nighttime was particularly difficult for me. I struggled greatly with surrendering to rest. I was afraid that while asleep, I wouldn't know how to fight, and God would take me home. On those nights where fear defeated rest, I called my friend Gary. Gary and I had met on a flight from Detroit to San Antonio. I was on my way to see my bestie Tex, and Gary was headed home. I was blessed to be seated next to him on that nonstop journey. Our conversation started when I noticed the beautiful ruby ring he was wearing. I felt drawn to him, as if I was being nudged. Gary appeared to have no interest in engaging in a conversation with me until I asked him about his ring. He explained that the beautiful ruby was a gift from his late wife of forty-two years,

Lindie. Our conversation took flight as we talked about life, love, and loss. Gary's face lit up while he shared stories about his beloved Lindie. His love and devotion for her was so obvious, it was almost tangible. Before landing in San Antonio, we exchanged our contact info.

Sadly, Gary was later diagnosed with cancer and underwent chemotherapy. During his battle with cancer, he was one of the few people I confided in about my illness. Our late-night calls were a blessing for us both. I believe I was nudged to talk to him on that flight because someone up above knew that we were going to need each other. The good Lord healed Gary. He beat his battle with cancer and has become one of my dearest friends and closest confidants. Ours is a beautiful friendship, formed among the clouds, two kindred spirits who have never embraced on solid ground. Isn't God amazing?

While keeping my health battles a secret from the rest of the world, I found myself in a dark place. I was feeling alone in the shadows when the bright light of my pageant past came back into my life. In my lonely hospital room, I reflected on a better place and time; my thoughts took me back to my pageant days.

Late one night, I decided to send a thank-you message to former Miss USA 2004, Shandi Finnessey. She was crowned Miss USA the year before I competed. I greatly admired her as I was reaching for my ultimate goal of competing on the same national stage. She was an inspiration to me back then, and I wanted to express my gratitude.

I was shocked when I received a quick response from the former Miss USA, who had also competed on *Dancing with the Stars*. She was so warm and kind. I shared with her a little bit about my health crisis. She immediately got on the horn, reaching out to the pageant world, asking for prayers on my behalf. Within no time, thousands of letters and well-wishes poured in from all over the country. My secret was out. I could no longer hide from my agonizing reality. I used the encouraging letters as rewards, allowing myself to open five of them every time I made it through painful procedures and endless poking and prodding. They gave me something to look forward to.

Shandi also called her successor, Miss USA 2005, Chelsea Cooley. Chelsea and I competed for Miss USA the same year I was awarded Miss Congeniality, and she took home the prestigious crown. Chelsea and I had a very special connection during the weeks of competition but fell out of touch in the years that followed. She couldn't believe the news of my failing health and immediately reached out to me by phone. Hearing Chelsea's voice again was music to my ears. God's army showed up in the form of beauty queens, a bond of sisterhood that couldn't be broken.

Chelsea took it upon herself to start a scholarship fund-raiser for Jack through an organization that she learned about while attending one of many functions at Trump Tower.

"As a parent, there are a lot of struggles and worries that we consume ourselves with. Melissa is enduring more than I can ever imagine. We often worry about our children's future. Please help me ease this stress for Melissa. Like Melissa, we can be brave for Jack" (Chelsea Cooley, Miss USA 2005).

When Abbey Curran, Miss Iowa USA 2008 and founder of the Miss You Can Do It pageant (a national pageant for young girls and women with special needs and challenges), heard the news, she also stepped up in a big way. I was one of the judges for the Miss Iowa USA pageant when she competed. Abbey didn't just walk away with the title; she walked away with my heart. She went above and beyond for my sweet Jack and me, donating the entry fees from that year's Miss You Can Do It pageant to Jack's scholarship fund. She also sent him every toy you could imagine from the Disney Store. Abbey has one of the most beautiful souls. She's an inspiration to women all over the world, including me.

Miss Michigan USA 2005, Crystal Hayes, also had a little boy around Jack's age. As Midwestern girls, we became fast friends while competing alongside one another in the national pageant. As word of my failing health spread throughout the pageant community, Crystal was also in a transition, uprooting her life in Michigan for the bright lights of Hollywood. She made a generous donation to Jack's scholarship fund after the sale of her Midwest home. Crystal is obviously stunning in appearance, but it's what's on the inside that will leave you breathless.

Shandi then shared my story with Jennifer Vannatta-Fisher, Miss Kansas 1998. Jennifer happened to be the wife of JC Fisher, a classically trained vocalist and recording artist from the three-time Emmy Award–winning trio in *The Texas Tenors*. In just one day, JC Fisher wrote and recorded a touching song for Jack and me entitled "Forever—Love, Mommy."

"My wife saw this young woman compete in the 2005 Miss USA pageant, where she represented Wisconsin. She even took home the congeniality award and was clearly loved by the other contestants. In the years since this adventure, she has battled an illness and has fought a brave battle, and her greatest inspiration to do so is her little boy Jack. As her story has spread throughout the country, people have been inspired to pray for Melissa and Jack and support them in any way possible. This includes me. In just over an hour, I came up with this melody in honor of Melissa and Jack" (JC Fisher, *The Texas Tenors*).

The touching melody created by JC Fisher instantly became the song of our hearts. Jack refers to it as "our special song."

When there are moments where words fall short, Jack and I listen to "Forever—Love, Mommy," and it says it all.

John Vannatta Jr., JC Fisher's brother-in-law, also reached out through Shandi Finnessy. John Vannatta Jr. is an executive state director for the Miss Universe Organization. He shared my story with the wonderful folks at Lindenwood University in Saint Charles, Missouri. Lindenwood University gives scholarships to state title holders, and when they heard my story, they generously offered to step up and give my sweet Jack a renewable scholarship when he graduates from high school. The news of this tremendous blessing breathed life back into my spirit, easing my worries for Jack's future.

It's impossible to name each person who blessed our lives during that most difficult time, but I know who you are, and I will never forget you. Your selfless acts of caring and kindness are forever etched on my heart, and I pray that the blessings return to you in abundance.

This was another example of God's purposeful plan for my life. By his amazing grace, I achieved my "impossible childhood dream" of competing in the Miss USA pageant, a blessing that allowed me to cross paths with these beautiful souls.

The outpouring of love and support from my pageant family and people around the world touched the deepest part of my soul. My immense gratitude was so overwhelming that I couldn't adequately express it; words wouldn't suffice. I had never been on the receiving end of such acts of kindness. I felt unworthy of their generosity. I could give 100 percent of myself to others but couldn't accept anything in return. I appeared to be a confident woman on the outside who had accomplished a lot, but on the inside, I was still the little girl whose self-worth never made it out of the church that turned me away or the attic where I slept after being beaten by my foster father. Now there were so many incredible people rising on my behalf, but I didn't have the tools to receive it.

Upon reflection, I see how my feelings of inadequacy unconsciously pushed some of those people away. I could receive the blessings for my sweet Jack but not for myself. I didn't know how, and for that, I humbly ask for forgiveness. And to everyone who lifted us in prayer, God heard you loud and clear.

Chapter 24

THE ATTEMPT TO EXTINGUISH MY LIGHT

B roke and unable to afford the top-notch care at the Mayo Clinic, due to the stipulations in my health insurance coverage, I was forced to rely on the hospital that dropped the ball during and after my pregnancy. I was left with an incurable illness that hijacked every part of my body and ransacked my quality of life, reducing me to relying on IV bags for survival.

Because of my orthostatic intolerance and hypovolemia, I needed to receive at least two liters of sodium chloride per day to maintain a certain level of blood volume, enough so I could sit up or stand without passing out. Research studies showed that I use about six hundred times more adrenaline upon standing than the average person. With the diagnosis of hyperadrenergic POTS and dysautonomia, gravity is not my friend. In the upright position, my blood drops and pools in my abdomen and feet, and then there is not enough blood pumping to my brain. My heart that is already overworking has to work even harder when I'm upright, pumping nearly two hundred beats per minute just to get blood to my brain, and if it doesn't, I pass out, which happens often. I was also in acute renal failure, so the two liters of IV fluids each day was also necessary to keep my kidneys working and prevent me from hitting the floor.

The physician caring for me at the time kept writing standing orders for my daily infusions. I wasn't in an infusion room; I was in a hospital room because I needed to lie down and was supposed to be closely monitored while adjusting to the change in blood volume.

Early on, when my veins were still easily accessible, I would check into the hospital in the evening, get my IV fluids, and check out in the early hours of the morning. My goal was to get what I needed and then make it back into my bed before Jack woke up. This illness had robbed me enough; I wasn't going to allow it to infringe on our morning "Jack and Mommy time." The pain of being stuck on the sidelines of his little-boy adventures was indescribable. I didn't have the honor of volunteering at his school or attending his field trips. I watched him learn how to ride a bike through the view from my front window—fleeting moments that made their way to the corners of my eyes, piercing a hole in my heart and leaving a lump in my throat.

Naturally, over time, it became more difficult finding a place to secure an IV. Since my veins were used over and over for years, they were left collapsed and riddled with scar tissue. What began as a twenty-minute task to get my IV started eventually turned into four to five hours of tortuous poking and prodding at any visible vein in my body. They could no longer run the IV pump at a rate of two hundred; it now was reduced to a rate of fifty, or my veins would blow, and we would have to start all over again. I could no longer receive what I needed. Using a vein finder, a cool new invention at the time, the doctors and nurses were in complete disbelief at what they saw. The scar tissue on my veins looked like noodles, covering my arms, legs, neck, and feet.

The IV hydration that improved my orthostatic intolerance and syncope was becoming nearly impossible to receive intravenously. The volume depletion exacerbated the hyperadrenergic state of my brain, making everything "hyper." My rapid gastric emptying became so severe that within five to seven minutes of ingesting food, my body would reject it, causing me to painfully projectile vomit.

Every vein had been used, causing irreversible damage. My body was wasting away. I was losing massive amounts of weight because I couldn't keep anything in. All that was left to vomit was blood.

The events that took place over the following nine weeks, after being unable to take in nourishment and adequate hydration, were a living hell. This is the story of how the devil took control of the medical facility and staff in charge of my well-being, an example of how they protected themselves, their pocketbook, and their reputation over a patient in need—a war between right and wrong, good and evil, and life and death.

I went from weighing 125 pounds to 89 pounds wrapped in a blanket. They never ordered a feeding tube, PICC line catheter, or port. I was starving to death without any meaningful medical intervention. There was no attempt to save my life. I was in a dark room at the end of a long hallway. I was alone and scared. I was severely malnourished and dehydrated; I had stopped urinating and was disappearing underneath the pink quilt gifted to me by a church that I had never attended. The medical staff was going long periods without checking on me.

My visits from Jack were getting less and less frequent because my feeble appearance was upsetting to him. I had worked so hard since he was a baby for him to engage and maintain eye contact with me, and here he was, a young boy, and I was so weak, I could barely sit up to hug him. On his visits to the hospital, he stopped looking at me. It took all my strength to whisper to him, "Eyes on Mommy, Jack."

With his attention focused toward the hospital-room window, he replied, "I can't look at you, Mommy. Your eyes aren't blue anymore. They're black."

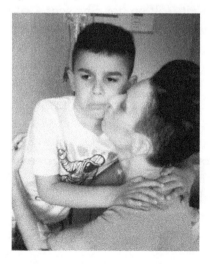

That one sentence broke my heart into a million pieces because they took that from him. They took my light away from him. Their neglect had taken so much from me when he was born, and I swore I wouldn't let them take my spirit because that belonged to Jack. And now they had taken what Jack could see of my spirit; it was through my eyes. His world existed through my bright blue eyes, and now all he could see was black. I didn't want him to remember me like that. I just wanted to live for him. I wasn't ready to go because they hadn't explored or attempted the options to save my life. I needed them to do better. I didn't know how to make sense of it, so just like I did as a little girl, I turned to Jesus, who loved me so much that he left his throne for the cross. When I couldn't understand my own suffering, I just pictured the nails through his hands, the innocent blood shed for me and my sins.

As the days and weeks passed by, still with no orders for a feeding tube, port, or PICC line, I was clearly dying. Who was going to save me? My family had fallen apart years earlier after the traumatic events that took place in the delivery room. The situation was too painful for them to bear. Along with Sergio, they shifted all their energy toward Jack. My mother practically lived at our home, sleeping on Jack's bedroom floor on nights when Sergio had to leave for work.

There was a kind nurse who was obviously struggling with the neglect that was unfolding before her eyes. The conflict between doing what's right and keeping the job that feeds your family was taking its toll on her. She sent a late-night text telling Sergio that he should get me out of there and take me to another hospital, somewhere that would help me. Sergio was so removed from the reality of what was happening; his head was buried so far in the sand because he didn't have the tools to cope. He didn't follow the nurse's plea. He couldn't give me what he didn't have.

In the weeks prior to my rapid decline, I developed a friendship with Jack's kindergarten teacher, Deb. During that time, we had deep conversations about life and death. I explained to her how my maternal grandfather, Cliff, had a special relationship with the priest in the small town where my mother grew up. I also shared with her the story about how when my grandfather passed, we took Jack to the cemetery to lay flowers and pay our respects. As the gates of the Catholic cemetery opened, his big brown eyes lit up. He squeezed my hand so tight and said, "Look, Mommy. This is the magic kingdom." He thought this cemetery was the most beautiful place on earth. I knew in that very moment, when the good Lord called me home, I had to be laid to rest in the "magic kingdom" for Jack. I also expressed to her my concerns about obtaining a cemetery plot there because I had walked away from the Catholic church when I was a little girl, after my family was given the tent. I hadn't done the work. What if they didn't think I was worthy of being buried there? Unbeknownst to me, Deb was taking notes. In the weeks following our conversation, Deb took it upon herself to email Father Joseph, the priest that was so close to my family, asking him to reach out to me, insisting that I needed his attention and prayers. She also informed him of my wish; after all, the cemetery—or "magic kingdom," as Jack referred to it—belonged to the church where he was the parish priest.

Father Joseph and I had only met briefly at my grandfather's funeral, but he knew a lot about me from the stories my grandfather shared with him over the years. When he opened Deb's email, he felt the deep concern coming from her words.

The next day, Father Joseph decided to make the forty-minute journey to the hospital where Deb said I would be. Dressed in casual attire, not his usual clerical garment, he wandered around the old Catholic hospital under the radar. A helpful custodian finally directed him to the last room at the end of a long hallway. What happened next was something Father Joseph said would stay with him forever.

"I cannot forget our first encounter in the hospital. I had to turn on the lights. It was dark in there. Melissa was under a blanket. She didn't appear to be alive until she looked up at me. There was an IV next to her, but it wasn't dripping. I touched her skin. It was cold and dry. There was darkness in the room, sad darkness everywhere."

Having been at the bedside of hundreds of people as they were at death's door, Father Joseph believed that I had just hours to live, so he called Sergio from the number listed "husband" in my cell phone. While Sergio was on his way to the hospital, Father Joseph held my hand and tried to comfort me. He knelt beside me and began weeping. He apologized for not getting to me sooner, crying out, "Please forgive me, please forgive me." He then prayed for me and for himself.

A short time later, Sergio entered the room. In his hand was an envelope that had been delivered to our home earlier that morning, with a note attached that read, "Must be delivered by 8 AM." For some reason, Sergio felt that the envelope addressed to me was important enough to bring to the hospital in that critical moment, and his instinct would prove to be right.

When Father Joseph let go of my hand to greet Sergio, the skin from my palm came off like a glove. Both men were shocked at the sight of my skin still attached to Father Joseph's hand after he pulled away.

He embraced Sergio with a hug, and they both broke down in tears. I don't know if it was seeing the priest at my bedside that snapped Sergio out of it or what, but for the first time in years, Sergio seemed to be feeling what was happening in the present moment. Through his tears, he dialed my cousin Mike, who had been calling our home for updates.

My cousin Mike and I had a special relationship. I babysat for him when he was a little boy. Now a man and home from college, he was worried when he heard the news of my failing health. Mike said he would be on his way immediately.

Then Sergio called my dear friend and pageant sister Chelsea Cooley in North Carolina. Chelsea was really concerned as to why I hadn't been returning her calls over the past several weeks. When Chelsea picked up, I heard Sergio say in what he thought was a whisper, "Chelsea, the priest is here. He doesn't think she has long to live. She's going to receive her last rights."

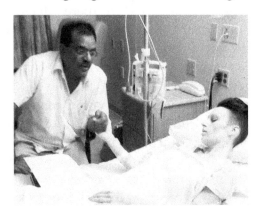

When my cousin Mike arrived and took one look at my wasted body, he raised his voice in anger and disbelief.

"Why the hell isn't anyone here helping her? How did things get this bad?"

Since Father Joseph had arrived earlier that day, not one nurse or hospital staff member had checked on me. It wasn't until my cousin raised his voice in the hallway, demanding an explanation, that the nurses entered my room. They had no idea that I had any visitors at this time. They appeared very nervous and anxious at the site of the men. They recognized Sergio from his visits with Jack. Sergio wasn't a threat to them; he never asked questions, he barely ever said a word, and he walked with his head down. As far as they were concerned, I was going to die there, no questions asked. The presence of the two unfamiliar men, Father Joseph and my cousin Mike, caught them off guard. It wasn't until Father Joseph pulled out his Bible, preparing to give me my last rights, that the nurses realized he was a man of the cloth. This made them extremely antsy. They told him to hurry up and then used the excuse that they needed to move me to a different room and prepare my room for a new patient. This was not true. I had been left in that room the whole time; there was no one to take my place. The priest could see right through them and their hasty lies.

Father Joseph proceeded to give me my last rights. He put the host in my mouth but had to pull it out minutes later because it never dissolved. I had no saliva. No one could see that I was crying; there was no moisture left to expel, not a single teardrop. He then leaned in and spoke directly to me. He explained that he came to see me that day because he had received an urgent email from Jack's kindergarten teacher. He said, "She must love you a lot because it was one of the longest emails I've ever received about visiting someone in the hospital." He further explained, "You don't have to worry about earning a plot in the cemetery. You earned that spot by living a life that was pleasing to God."

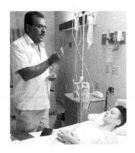 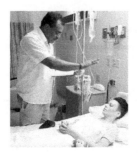 

He then handed Sergio two sheets of paper confirming that the cemetery plot located diagonally from my grandparents Cliff and Nancy now belonged to me. My feet would lay at the head of my beloved grandmother, in the "magic kingdom," for Jack. At that moment, my spirit gifted me with enough strength to gently squeeze his hand and humbly whisper the words, "Thank you."

The father and my cousin Mike then said their mournful goodbyes. Mike said on his way out, "I will be back tomorrow. Promise me that you won't leave me." There was no one who wanted to make good on that promise more than me.

I didn't want to die there. They had taken enough from me and my sweet Jack. I had chosen forgiveness over a payout for the unfortunate oversights and events that took place during and after my pregnancy, but they still viewed me as a threat. And when my veins were all used up, they decided not to attempt any form of medical intervention.

It's inconceivable for anyone, in this day and age, with all the advances in medical technology, to die of malnutrition and dehydration while under the care of medical professionals. Not one attempt was made to save my life. I don't care if you are a drug addict on the street or the president of a *Fortune* 500 company, each life is valuable and deserves to be treated as such. I was a good person, a daughter, a sister, a friend, a wife, and most of all, a mother—a mother who paid the ultimate price to give life—and all I wanted was the honor of watching my little boy grow up. I wasn't seeking compensation for the loss of my once-healthy body or promising future. I was just trying to get the IV hydration and nutrition I so desperately needed to make it through each day, nothing more.

The outpouring of love that I was now receiving from people all over the country, noticeable by the hundreds of unopened letters in my hospital room, left me overwhelmed with gratitude. It also put me in a vulnerable position with the facility in which I was receiving care.

Unfortunately, to them I was just someone who could jeopardize their reputation. If I lived, I could talk. They wanted me to hurry up and die already. The only problem with that was, it wasn't up to them. You see, the devil can bring us to the doors of death, but he cannot kill us. Only God can open *that* door. He gives us our first breath, and he is in charge of our last.

It was just Sergio and I left in the room; he was sitting in a chair with his head down, holding the papers Father Joseph had given him. He was staring at the one with a square highlighted in bright yellow, indicating where my plot was located. He finally set the papers down, walked over, and picked up the large shiny envelope that he had brought with him to the hospital that day.

The envelope was addressed to me with a Trump Tower, New York City, return address. Standing at the foot of my bed, Sergio proceeded to open the envelope. Inside was a beautiful vanilla card with gold italic writing: "From the office of Donald J. Trump." Behind the card was a glossy photo of the then billionaire real estate mogul, television star, and owner of the Miss Universe pageant. Handwritten on the photograph, in his signature gold color, was the message, "To Melissa—one of the BRAVEST women I know. Best wishes, Donald J. Trump."

After Sergio read the message out loud, he set the envelope down on the hospital tray next to my bed and then kissed my forehead goodbye. As the door shut behind him, like rewinding a movie, a lifetime of memories replayed through my mind. It was all there—being born into severe poverty, my tiny foot falling through the icy lake on my way to school, being homeless, living in abusive foster homes, achieving my "impossible" childhood dream of becoming Miss Wisconsin, making history in the Miss USA pageant, giving back to the church that turned me away, my wedding day, the miracle birth of my precious son, receiving my last rights, and the unsolicited handwritten note from Donald J. Trump, "To one of the BRAVEST women I know." His powerful words gave me another clear mission—to keep fighting.

The kind gesture from Mr. Trump was the fuel that my spirit needed. The fact that a man I had admired all my life took the time from his busy schedule to think of me many years after our meeting on the Miss USA stage, a message that said "Must be delivered by 8 AM" on the day I would receive my last rights, was another sign of God's perfect timing. It ignited the light within me, a light that was being extinguished too soon.

My body was slipping away, but my spirit was on fire. There was a clear separation between the two, body and spirit. The only pulse detected was coming from a pulse oximeter on my earlobe. My cousin Mike had placed my bed at a forty-degree angle because I had been choking on my own blood. My body wore the appearance of death, but my spirit remained bright, untouched, and filled with overwhelming gratitude. Somehow, I had holy confidence that God had more for me to do, somewhere beyond the dark space in which my body lay.

When Deb heard the news of Father Joseph's visit the day before, she repeatedly called the hospital in hopes of receiving an update. They kept telling her that they didn't have a patient there under my name. How kind of them to uphold the patient-privacy laws while failing to uphold the ethical standards of the Hippocratic oath.

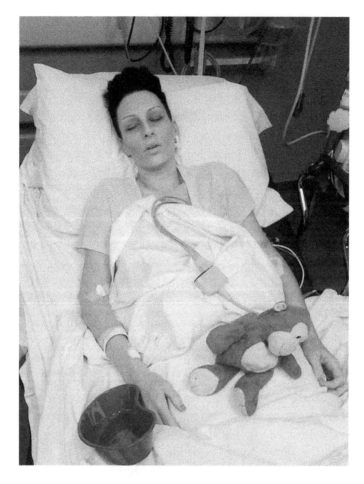

Despite their denial of me being there, Deb came anyway. When she opened the door to my room, she was in such shock at the sight of me, it caused her to feel sick. Always a take-charge kind of person, she had to do something to try to help me. Deb is a thin woman but also strong; she was able to put me into a wheelchair that was left in the hallway. She then wheeled me out of there and put me into her minivan. She drove for about thirty minutes to the office of a well-respected doctor of internal medicine who also specializes in nutrition. She pulled her van up as close as she could to the front doors and ran into the doctor's office. She asked the ladies at the front desk for a wheelchair. She quickly returned to the van, where I was laid back in the seat, with the wheelchair and a receptionist following behind her. They helped me into the chair and wheeled me into the office.

When the compassionate doctor took one look at me, he appeared to be in a state of confusion and shock. He asked a series of rapid-fire questions. He didn't know my medical history; he just saw a young woman lying in front of him who looked like death. Deb explained that I was coming from a particular hospital and had been suffering from autonomic failure and that I wasn't able to take in any nutrition for the past nine weeks, and nothing was being done about it. The concerned doctor questioned, "She's coming from a hospital?" He was in disbelief as if I was being held somewhere and a crime was being committed, finding it hard to believe that I was under a hospital's care. He told Deb that if I was truly coming from that hospital, she needed to take me back there immediately. Feeling helpless and not knowing what else to do, she reluctantly drove me back.

Deb once again pulled up to the doors and placed me into a wheelchair. We took the elevator to the correct floor, and she pushed me back to the room at the end of the long hallway. She put me into bed and draped the pink quilt over my body. My absence went completely unnoticed by the staff, a clear indication of how often I was being checked on. I felt like I was being brought to my death, that Deb was going to be the last person I saw on earth. I wondered if she would ever share this story with Jack, the story of how she took me to get help and how I had to return without any, the story of the day his mother died.

As she sat next to me, gently rubbing the top of my hand with tears welling up in her eyes, I wanted to thank her for being so good to my sweet Jack, for reaching out to Father Joseph and securing my spot in the magic kingdom, and for taking me that day on my last adventure in search of a miracle.

About a half hour after our stealthy return, Deb and I locked eyes when we heard a familiar voice coming from down the hallway. It was music to our ears, the sound of the gentle voice belonging to the doctor we had just visited. Unable to shake the image of what he saw in his office and feeling the need to investigate for himself, he canceled the rest of his appointments for the day and drove to the hospital where she claimed I was. When he opened the door and saw me with his own eyes, lying there in a room I had obviously been in for some time, his kind and gentle tone of voice quickly changed as he backed out of the room and into the hallway.

"I need to see Ms. Young's medical file now!" he demanded. "She needs a PICC line put in immediately!" I could hear the staff frantically running around. He then ordered the procedure to take place in the first available operating room. I was now a patient whose life had value under the care of an empathetic doctor determined to save it.

There wasn't enough time for Sergio to get there before I was taken to the OR, where a PICC line catheter was inserted into my left arm. When they flushed the line with saline for the first time, I had a metallic-like taste in the back of my mouth, a clear sign that we had a winner.

My new doctor and lifesaver immediately started me on TPN (total parenteral nutrition), a method used when a person cannot receive feedings or fluids by mouth. He ordered it to run twenty-four hours a day. I would now receive around-the-clock nutrition and hydration through my new catheter. His greatest worry was my risk of developing refeeding syndrome. Refeeding syndrome is a complication that can occur when food is reintroduced to patients who are starved or severely malnourished.

In the days that followed, my new doctor stopped in to check on me frequently. As I began to regain some strength from the nonstop nutrients, I expressed to him that I did not want to be there any longer and that I never wanted to step foot in that place again. He agreed and promised I wouldn't have to return. He set me up with home health care and visiting nurses and promised if I needed to go to a hospital for any reason, it would be one of my choosing. Through the fearless courage of an angel disguised as a kindergarten teacher and an outside doctor's compassion and quick actions, I was blessed with more moments with my sweet Jack. I would finally be heading home, away from the place that had underestimated God almighty and the power of his mercy and grace.

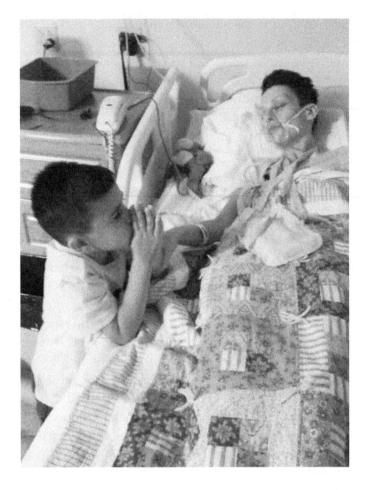

Then and now, I continue to pray for the people who overlooked my illness and later tried to cover it up by withholding basic needs and waiting for me to die. I figure they need the prayers more than I. The human spirit is so powerful; unlike our bodies, it's not easy to break. I choose gratitude and forgiveness over anger and bitterness. This allows me to see and appreciate the beauty and blessings in most everything. Along with my faith in God, my fierce devotion for Jack, and encouragement from my friend Donald J. Trump that came in the form of a personalized letter, "To one of the BRAVEST women I know," I was reminded that the smallest acts of caring and kindness could turn a life around. Mine is proof of that.

Chapter 25

LIVING WITH INTENTION

S aved by grace, I was greeted at home by my loved ones and the kindhearted nurses that would be caring for me there. I was back in my own room just down the hall from my sweet Jack. Next to my bed was an IV pole. Attached to it were a pump and a large heavy bag of nutrients that would run through my PICC line and into my body continuously.

My dear friend and pageant sister Chelsea Cooley flew from North Carolina to my home in Wisconsin to comfort me and assist with my care. I managed to carry the heavy IV bag and pump in a backpack on my back to surprise her at the airport. It took everything I had, but it was well worth it. Not long before then, I thought I'd never see her again. Our reunion was nothing short of beautiful, bringing us both to tears.

Chelsea was a sight for sore eyes. She jumped right in, learning from the nurses how to infuse my IV bags with the correct amount of nutrients, flush the PICC line in between and control the digital pump. If I didn't know any better, I would have thought that the former Miss USA had also attended nursing school. She was very gentle with strong attention to detail.

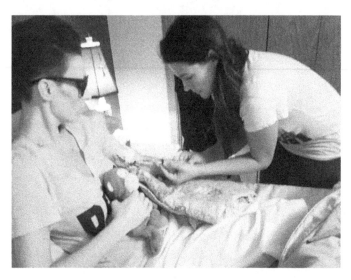

Chelsea also developed a special bond with my sweet Jack. He was in love with her from the moment he saw her, but then again, what young boy wouldn't be? For Jack, it went deeper than her obvious beauty. She was attentive and engaged. She would get down on the floor to play with him and read books.

Even with the medical intervention, it took a huge toll on what was left of my body. The PICC line catheter was just a temporary fix for my lifelong, incurable condition. It was just the Band-Aid on my bullet wound. Either way, it saved me in my last moments of life, and for that, I was eternally grateful for its blessing.

The horrific situation that had taken place gave me a new perspective on life and death and who I would want in charge of my well-being if, for some reason, I couldn't make those decisions for myself. With a heavy heart, I found myself staring at a clipboard with a booklet of papers attached. For two hours, as I fumbled with the pen between my fingers, I spoke to God. My faith in him was stronger than ever, and my faith in the medical system was no longer. I knew what I had to do. I slowly put my signature at the bottom of the page entitled "Do Not Resuscitate." The paperwork was then faxed to my doctor where he placed his signature as well. The only one I could trust with my life was the one who gave it to me, God Almighty.

Eventually, my first PICC line formed a blood clot and needed to be replaced. Still needing to receive around-the-clock TPN feedings and daily hydration, I was advised by my doctor to try a port. A port-a-catheter is a medical device attached to a flexible tube that is threaded into a large vein above the right side of the heart. Placed under the skin, it can serve as a better alternative for receiving long-term infusions.

On the day of the procedure, I was understandably nervous, but I was desperate and would try anything that was offered, especially after barely surviving a situation where I received no options. My new doctor was amazing and looking out for my best interest in the long term. Chelsea and my mother were there for me, waiting outside of the OR as the procedure got underway.

The anesthesiologist asked me to count down from ten as he was putting me under anesthesia. Instead of counting down, I used the few seconds to make a plea: "I have a son who needs me . . ." And that was it—I was out. The next thing I knew, my eyes opened to a very bright light, and I could hear the most painful, bloodcurdling screams coming from somewhere nearby. My eyeballs moved back and forth as I tried to make sense of what was going on. Unbeknownst to me, at the same time, Chelsea and my mother could hear the same bloodcurdling screams from as far away as the hospital waiting room. They said that they panicked because they immediately identified who it was coming from. The horrifying screams that I was trying to make sense of while waking up from anesthesia were coming from me. Something had gone terribly wrong.

The staff wheeled me out of the OR to the room where Chelsea and my mother were anxiously waiting for me with tears in their eyes. The screams followed down the hall as I made my way to them. Chelsea immediately demanded that the surgeon inject something for pain through the new PICC line they had placed in the other arm before the procedure. My mother was frantically pacing the floor, overcome by a flood of emotions and the memories from my nightmare delivery. After receiving the pain medication, the surgeon explained that things didn't go as planned. No kidding!

During the procedure, they had to try twice, putting a port in and taking it out, putting another one in and having to leave it there or I would bleed out. After a lot of manipulating, the port was not positioned correctly and not accessible for my daily feedings and hydration. The painful experience was for nothing. The device was protruding out of the side of my neck and bulging from my skin. The port was too large for my still-malnourished body. A pediatric port would have been the correct option for someone in my condition, but it was too late. What was done was done.

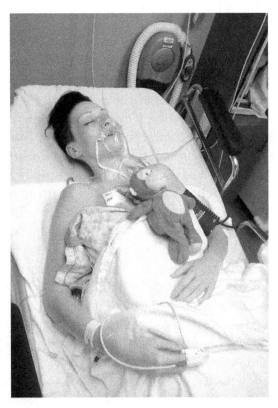

I would have to leave the large, inaccessible port in my body for the next fifteen days to allow some healing before it could be removed. The pain during those fifteen days was indescribable. Unfortunately, Chelsea had to return home during that time and wouldn't be able to accompany me to the removal procedure. Once again, Chelsea called in her troops.

My dear friend and former Miss Wisconsin USA Bishara Dorre stayed by my side for days. Concerned about my pain and the position I would be left in for the next two weeks, Bishara questioned the surgeon who performed the failed procedure. The surgeon explained that what happened to me in the operating room that day was a one-in-a-million circumstance. By then, I had heard that expression so often, I thought it would be a good idea to start playing the lottery. As luck would have it, I'm still waiting on a jackpot. Not knowing what else to say, the surgeon then asked if she could pray for me. In my defense, Bishara swiftly snapped back in what seemed like one breath: "Pray for her? She's got a thousand letters under her bed of people praying for her! You need to get in there and cut Ms. Lady!" They say laughter is the best medicine, and a dose of Bishara was the perfect prescription that I needed. Forgive me, Lord, but I still giggle thinking about the look on that surgeon's face when Bishara put her in her place.

My poor doctor who had suggested the port and ordered the usually easy procedure had never experienced or anticipated a complication like that to take place. In fact, ever since then, my doctor and I don't say the word "port." We call it the "P-word," and that's enough. We both know what we're talking about. He agreed that we would move on to other options, and the P-word is something we would never try again.

I was nervous before the initial insertion procedure so you can only imagine how I felt about the removal fifteen days later. For two weeks, I was stuck holding my head in one position. If I moved my head or neck to the left, there wasn't enough skin to pull over the ill-fitted device underneath.

As soon as my bestie Kelly Hall (Tex) heard about the events that unfolded and the upcoming procedure, she booked a flight from her home in San Antonio to Wisconsin. She was determined to be by my side. Just like always, she was there when I needed her the most. There's a famous quote by Walter Winchell that reads, "A real friend is one who walks in when the rest of the world walks out." Well, that would be my Tex. While I was being prepped for the port removal procedure, we recited lines from our favorite movie *Fried Green Tomatoes*. As they wheeled me to the OR, Tex shouted, "Towanda!" Now, if you haven't seen the movie before, Towanda is a name referred to by the main characters when they do something daring or brave. It's like an alter ego, "Towanda the Avenger!" Tex knew just how to calm my nerves and make me giggle, another clear reason why she's one of my dearest friends.

Thank heavens, the procedure went perfect. The port was finally removed. The only thing left was a very noticeable scar. I even joked about getting a tattoo there that reads, "I paid for a port, and all I got was this gnarly scar."

Even though my new doctor, the one who ordered my life-saving PICC line, kept his promise about me not having to return to the hospital where he found me, I was left severely traumatized. Just the thought of entering any medical facility brought up feelings of panic, fear, and distrust. I was receiving excellent care from my visiting nurses at home, but there were certain procedures that still had to be done at a hospital. So naturally, I chose a hospital in the complete opposite direction of the facility I feared. It was there where God sent in one of his brightest souls to regain my faith in the medical profession. Of all people, the vice president of patient care would show me a different side of the profession that left scar tissue on every part of me, physically and emotionally.

I was in between PICC line procedures, and the nurses at the hospital would need to access my very poor veins for hydration. After an hour of failed attempts to secure an IV, they said, "Let's call Denise. She's the very best." As we waited, the nurses seemed to want to make everything perfect for her arrival. I could sense that Denise was someone of authority and the nurses had great respect for the woman they called "the very best." A short time later, I heard the fast-paced clicking of high heels approaching my hospital room. I tensed up as the nurse said, "That's her coming." I sent up a silent prayer, "Please, God, let her have mercy on me."

The door opened, and there stood a very bright light and an aura of goodness. I had only experienced this one time before in my life. It came on the day I was saved by my foster mother, Joyce. I immediately recognized the blessing of this moment, just like I did as a child. Denise walked over to me, and the light followed. Her smile was radiant, and her beautiful eyes were kind. I explained to her a little bit about the hell I had been through and why I didn't have any good veins left. The other nurses excused themselves, and it was just her and me left in the room. The touch of her warm hands put my nerves at ease, and my fear dissipated. I knew I was in the presence of somebody extraordinary.

As she held my hand, she reassured me that we would get through this together, that she wouldn't give up on me, and that we would only quit if I wanted to. It was the first time since my return from the Mayo Clinic that I felt like somebody in her position was my ally. It also helped that she laughed at my inappropriate jokes.

Denise was able to do what no other nurse, doctor, or anesthesiologist could for years. She secured an IV on her first try. It's like the scar tissue faded away, and my veins came out of hiding just for her. From that day forward, Denise has been my angel in a lab coat. She would miss important meetings to make sure I am receiving what I need. She has entered the OR while I was undergoing a procedure to check on my well-being. I know the horrific neglect that brought me to the doors of death and caused irreversible damage and suffering that never would have happened under her watchful eye. She repaired that place inside of me that had lost faith in her profession's humanity. Now, when I hear the clicking of those high heels approaching my hospital room, instead of praying for God's protection, I am at peace knowing He is sending me one of His most merciful soldiers.

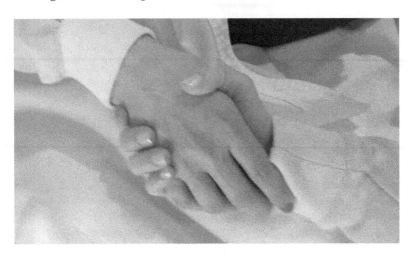

Since Jack's birth, I have been ill. He has never known me any different. Several months ago, I had an experience with Jack that sums everything up. I have an IV pole next to my bed at home with a hydration bag hanging from it.

Every once in a while, for the past few years, my sweet Jack would ask out of the blue to anybody, "Does your mommy have fishies in her fishy tank?" No matter what answer he received, he followed up by saying, "My mommy has no fishies in her fishy tank." We never knew what he meant. I explained to him numerous times that I never owned a fish tank. He would say, "Yes, you do, Mommy. You just don't have fishies." I had no idea where this was coming from. I thought maybe it was from a movie or something.

One night, when I wasn't well enough to tuck Jack into bed, he said, "That's okay, Mommy. I will tuck you in tonight." He pulled the blankets over me, all the way up to my eyeballs. After we said our prayers, he kissed my forehead, and before leaving the room, he gave my IV bag a gentle squeeze and whispered to himself, "Yep, still no fishies in her fishy tank."

I realized in that moment, Jack never saw me as being sick; he didn't know any different. He thought my IV bag was a fish tank. All this time, I was beating myself up about having all the medical equipment in my home because I was concerned about Jack worrying about my health and realizing that my circumstances were different from other mothers, but he didn't. In his own mind, he made up something very sweet and innocent about the medical equipment. It wasn't foreign or scary to him like I feared it would be. For the first time, I failed to see the situation through Jack's eyes. My "mommy guilt" about bringing my medical equipment into his world was for nothing.

When my nurse arrived the next morning, I shared with her how I finally understood the story of Jack and my fish tank. She said, "We are going to fix it!" So she printed off and laminated a goldfish pattern with a blue water background and custom fit it to hang over the back of my IV bag. She made it appear as if fish were swimming all around in there. That evening, while I was hooked up to the IV, Jack came into my room to snuggle with me. I will never forget the joy on his face when he looked over at my transformed IV bag. Jumping for joy, he shouted over and over, "Mommy, you have fishies in your fishy tank!" His heart was so happy. When he comes to visit me at the hospital, I take the insert to make sure his mommy is never without fishies in her fishy tank again.

I realized that Jack is handling my illness the same way I am. This is our life, and our glass is half full, not half empty. If it ever seems half empty, we pour it into a smaller glass because there are so many beautiful things for us to be thankful for, even in our circumstances. If I were told today that I could be 100 percent healed and have a healthy, able body again but I'd have to take away all the lessons and blessings that this illness afforded me, I would say, "No way!" I would not make that deal. Maybe we won't have a lifetime together, but the quality of our time is priceless and meaningful, and for that, we are rich beyond measure. We understand that every moment is a blessing, and we don't overlook it.

I taught Jack from early on that "when you give a hug, you intend to show love. So you should show that by hugging me with intention, which feels like this." Then I would hug him with intention, and he would hug me back the same way. Recently, he was at the hospital, visiting me, when a physician came in and said, "Hello there," to Jack. Jack put his hand out to shake hands with the doctor and said, "Nice to meet you, Mr. Doctor, sir." The doctor mildly shook his hand, and Jack politely corrected him. "Excuse me, sir, we must shake hands with intention." Jack said, "Not with spaghetti arms." It was a great mommy moment for me because my child with autism taught the physician a lesson on how to shake hands with intention—the same boy who, we were told, wouldn't be capable of anything more than sitting in a circle.

When you believe in something so strong, it can provide you with the energy and strength needed when you don't have it. My circumstances with Jack while fighting for my life is a perfect example. I didn't have the energy to be so hands-on, making sure I was doing everything right by him. It's impossible to describe the effort it took, but I did it. When you love someone so much, the strength and energy just appear. It's so physical, but it's in your spirit, and that has the ability to carry you through. When something comes from a place of sheer love deep inside of you, in your spirit, your soul and your heart, its power can serve your physical body.

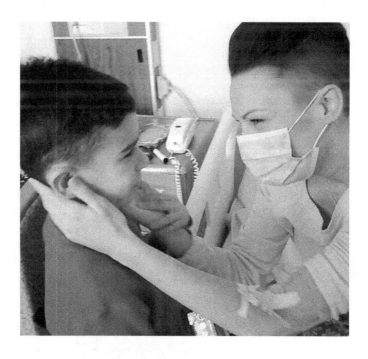

I have had thirteen PICC lines, a port, Hickman lines, and Groshong lines—four chest catheters, and still counting. I've had blood transfusions, cardiac ablations, and countless operations and tests, many experimental. I've been the subject of several medical research studies. I endure never-ending painful procedures and interventions day after day, constantly confounding all medical expectations for my survival.

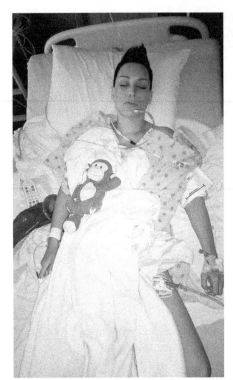
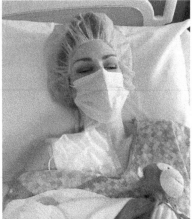
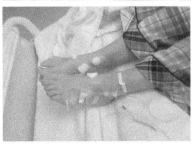

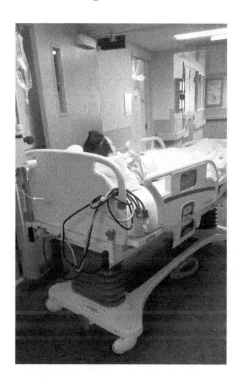

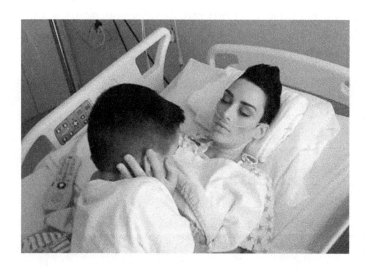

Recently, a doctor said to me, "There is no medical explanation as to how you are still alive." To this, I responded, "The keyword is *medical*." God only gives us a certain amount of time on this earth, and mine isn't up. I'm still here because, for some reason, He needs me to be. There must be more for me to do, and maybe this book is that thing. Writing the story of my life was both gut-wrenching and therapeutic. I'm not the same person who started typing the first chapters; I am forever changed by this process.

As a person who has always been painfully private, baring my soul and reliving each moment to share it with you was one of the most difficult things I've had to do. However, I was determined not to allow my life story to die with me, and now it won't. Jack is my legacy. I will live on through him and the pages of this memoir. A life lived and written by me.

Life has shown me things I never wanted to see pain and suffering I never wanted to experience it, but through it all, I rise up with a bold faith allowing nothing to break my spirit. There are adventures to be had, my favorite rock to sit on overlooking the lake and sunset with my name on it. There is a little boy who needs his mommy more than anything in the world, the same little boy who prays to God every night before falling asleep in his little blue bed. For him, I am a fierce warrior, embracing the incredible power within me, always getting back up, always sacrificing and overcoming. I am blessed, and I am grateful, never taking for granted the precious and fragile gift of being alive.

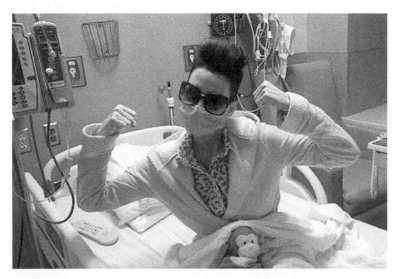

Chapter 26

FOR SUCH A TIME AS THIS

When Mr. Trump announced he was running for president, I asked God to please keep me here long enough to see it come to fruition. I vowed until my last breath that I would use this voice to speak up about who Mr. Trump really is. He is the most wonderful man I've ever met. He has a heart made of pure gold, a fighting spirit, and a fierce love for this great country.

On Monday, November 7, 2016, at 5:00 a.m., I unhooked from everything, including my IV hydration, left a note that read:

"Until my last breath . . ." and boarded a flight for New York City. On that nonstop journey to the Big Apple, I reflected on the seven months prior.

I had been a strong voice for Mr. Trump, even in some of my weakest moments. I traveled all over, from city to city, rally to rally, carrying a fifteen-pound IV bag and pump in a backpack. I appeared on dozens of national news shows, and when I wasn't well enough to make it to the studio, I was interviewed live from my hospital bed.

Nothing but death would have stopped me from extolling my heartfelt gratitude for Mr. Trump's kindness and compassion while at the same time refusing to be drawn into political conversations. As I said from the very beginning, my gratitude was personal, not political. Mr. Trump was there for me when I needed it the most, when all hope was lost, on the day I received my last rites.

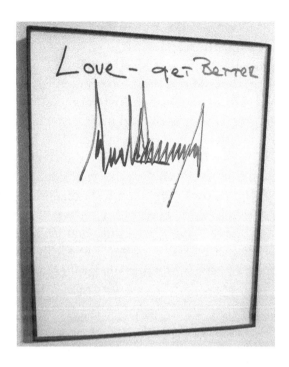

On Tuesday, November 8, 2016, with the loving support of two incredible women, Rose Tennent (radio show host) and Lauren (associate producer of the Hannity radio show), and my chest catheters taped down, nicely hidden beneath a long white jacket, I stood tall for over ten hours at Trump headquarters in New York City. As the ballots were being counted, my body felt like it was going to collapse, but my spirit and fellow patriots wouldn't allow it. They held me up, giving the appearance that I was levitating above the crowd. The camera zoomed in on my raw emotion as I learned, along with the rest of the world, our forty-fifth president of the United States of America was my hero, Mr. Donald J. Trump.

President-Elect Donald J. Trump held a thank-you event shortly after his historic election night victory. Unfortunately, my health wouldn't allow me to attend, but Tana Goertz was there. Once again, she was bold and brave on my behalf. She approached President-Elect Trump backstage just moments before he was scheduled to greet the massive adoring crowd. Tana took the opportunity and asked Mr. Trump if I could be her guest at the inaugural ball. He said, "Absolutely." She then confirmed, "Okay, I have your word on that." Mr. Trump responded, "Yes, let's give Melissa a call right now." The soon-to-be president then dialed my number, which he had saved in his phone. "Hello, love. How are you doing? I have Tana here, and I want to personally invite you to the inaugural ball. I want you there." Tana's son, Myles, snapped a photo of Mr. Trump and his mother making that call.

As inauguration day drew near, I received a package at my door from Washington DC. When I opened it, there were several envelopes with the golden inaugural seal on them with invitations requesting my presence to attend and participate at each of these historical events—the Make America Great Again welcome concert, the inauguration of Donald John Trump as president of the United States of America and Michael Richard Pence as vice president of the United States of America, the presidential inaugural parade, and the inaugural ball.

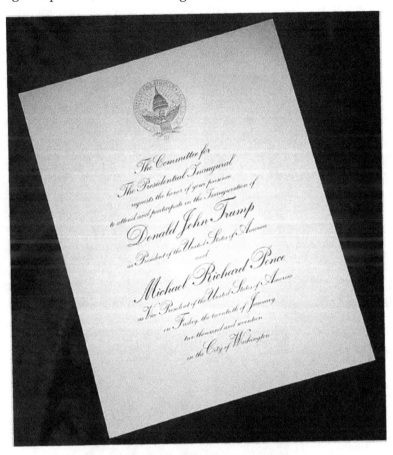

Dressed in a floor-length royal-blue velvet gown with jewels perfectly placed around my neck covering my exposed chest catheter, in the highest of heels, with my head held high and my knees shaking a bit, I walked into the inaugural ball. My spirit absorbing, my mind recording, and my heart appreciating each beat, each moment, each step.

A short time later, through a tiny slit in the curtain behind the celebrity-packed ballroom, Tana and I were waved over by the Secret Service and guided backstage, where no one else was permitted. As I stepped through the curtain, I found myself looking straight into the eyes of our new president and first lady.

President Trump and First Lady Melania greeted me with a warm embrace. "How are you feeling? How is your son doing?" asked President Trump.

Then he said, "Mike [talking to our new vice president], have you met Melissa?" Vice President Pence reached his hand out and, with a kind smile, said, "Karen and I have been praying for you."

After my warm meeting with the new vice president and just moments before they took the stage to dance together for all the world to see, President Trump asked me again, "How are you feeling? Do you need anything? Would you like someone to get you some juice?" As ever, he was so loving and thoughtful. Even in the greatest moments of his life, he was thinking of others, like myself.

Just like everyone else in the nation, I watched the first family dance at the inaugural ball. My view, however, was from a monitor behind the stage on which they were gracing. It was a priceless moment that money couldn't buy and fame couldn't afford. There was no golden ticket you could obtain. There was no position you could hold, an incomparable moment that only God and his grace could provide.

On that glorious evening in January of 2017, the poor little girl from Wisconsin who lost her shoe in the icy lake, who lived in a tent in a park, who struggled through foster homes, who had faced painful and endless medical procedures for years, constantly exceeding all medical expectations for her survival, was standing strong next to the new president and the first lady at the inaugural ball, the grandest ball on the world stage. Unlike Cinderella, I didn't have to worry about midnight approaching because the dream had already come true in more beautiful ways than I could have prayed for. Gratitude still wins the day.

Christmas 2018, I entered the White House and walked proud for that little girl who always daydreamed of a better life. It was more breathtaking than my dreams had ever allowed.

As I turned each corner and entered each room of the house that symbolizes democracy, freedom, and our great country's history, my elation was obvious to those around me; but whatever joy I was exuding on the outside, it felt a million times greater on the inside. Tears filled my eyes as I admired the portraits of President John F. Kennedy and First Lady Jacqueline Kennedy. A childhood dream turned reality, a moment that was nothing short of amazing grace. Oh, and of course, in place of that old half-eaten candy necklace, like Jackie, I wore pearls.

Melissa Young and her beloved son, Jack

About the Author

Melissa Young is Miss Wisconsin USA 2005 and was awarded the prestigious title of Miss Congeniality at the Miss USA pageant that year. She is the first woman from Wisconsin to earn that special award.

Hailing from a small Midwest town, Melissa has never let anything hold her back from chasing her dreams with passion and fortitude. After graduating from high school, she moved to Los Angeles, California, and diligently auditioned for acting roles, and she landed on a soap opera and numerous television commercials. Her determination, sense of humor, and magnetic personality have always drawn people in. Ever the fighter, coming from humble beginnings to God's purposeful path on the Miss USA stage, Melissa would forever be influenced and prepared by this journey for her greatest role and achievement in life—becoming a mother. Ten years ago, her precious son, Jack, entered the world. Melissa has been fighting for her life ever since. While this was preventable, her deep faith in God and forgiving spirit is touching millions around the globe.

The world-renowned Mayo Clinic has used her very rare and complex medical case for countless research studies. Thousands of supporters from around the world on social media follow her story as her sheer will to live for precious moments with her son is changing people's perspective on life forever.

Melissa became a media sensation after her public "thank you" to Donald J. Trump during the Wisconsin primaries went viral. His emotional support and encouragement during her darkest hour ignited the spark of hope within, lifting her lifeless body to its feet. She has been interviewed, extolling her immense gratitude on dozens of national news shows, including Fox's Sean Hannity, Stuart Varney & Company, On the Record with Greta Van Susteren, America's News HQ, CNN, and Inside Edition.

Melissa is a courageous warrior. There is no medical explanation as to how she is still alive. God's plan for her life is purposeful, and His miracles are abundant. Through it all, the love Melissa has for Jack and the grace she embodies is true beauty in its purest form.

CPSIA information can be obtained
at www.ICGtesting.com
Printed in the USA
BVHW031919170919
558677BV00001B/54/P

9 781941 049990